PHILADELPHIA
Food Crawls

Jacklin Altman

TOURING *the* NEIGHBORHOODS
ONE BITE *&* LIBATION *at a* TIME

G
Pe

GUILFORD

T0204472

Every establishment in this book was verified as being open at the time of publication, but it is always a good idea to make sure that is still the case before you go. Enjoy!

Globe
Pequot

An imprint of Globe Pequot, the trade division of The Rowman & Littlefield Publishing Group, Inc.
4501 Forbes Blvd., Ste. 200
Lanham, MD 20706
www.rowman.com

Distributed by NATIONAL BOOK NETWORK

Copyright © 2022 by Jacklin Altman

Photos by Jacklin Altman, with additional images provided with permission by: Angelos Pizzeria South Philly; Chestnut Hill Brewing Company; Diane Tamulavage + Charlie Jelke @floridaphoodies FKA fishtownfoodies; Genos Steaks; Joe Sobeck @philadelphia_photos (The Dutch); Josh Moore @josheatsphilly; Kevin Gross @phillyfoodguru; Lauren Carroll @love_phillyfood; Lexi Mestas @leximestas (The Dutch); Marina Kuhns @marina_eatss (Frankford Hall); Metropolitan Bakery/Cafe; Nick Deezy @eats_with_deezy; Pats King of Steaks; Royal Boucherie; The Dutch; Tiffany Tran; Woodrows Sandwich Shop; and Yamitsuki.

British Library Cataloguing in Publication Information Available

Library of Congress Cataloging-in-Publication Data Available

♾️™ The paper used in this publication meets the minimum requirements of American National Standard for Information Sciences—Permanence of Paper for Printed Library Materials, ANSI/NISO Z39.48-1992.

My love of food was fostered by my grandparents from an early age, and even though they've all gone to a better place, I like to think they'd be really proud of this book.

This book is dedicated to all of the friends, family, and amazing restaurant owners who helped make this project a reality. To my mom and dad, thank you for teaching me to try everything. To my friends and husband, thank you for eating a lot of cold meals so I could get the best picture.

To the city of Philadelphia, thank you for being so delicious.

Contents

Introduction

Philadelphia is so much more than just cheesesteaks and the football team that finally won a Super Bowl in 2018 (though we talk about both *a lot*). The city is rich in history (with a large cracked bell to prove it), and the food scene has been booming, with new restaurants, shops, and bakeries popping up year over year, bringing their own delicious flair to the city. A city that's seen as being relatively affordable for young people rent-wise, more and more people are flocking to Philadelphia, and new restaurants are on the rise because of it. The unpretentious food scene here means that chefs feel safe experimenting with new cuisines from around the world, and it gives rise to diverse and delicious dining experiences in the city's various neighborhoods. From one of the nation's most lauded fine-dining restaurants in Old City to the laid-back coffee shops throughout Fishtown, this is a city that truly does it all and does it well. So strap on some comfy shoes, put on whatever pants give you the most waistline leeway, and allow me to be your guide as you eat your way through the City of Brotherly Love.

Follow the Icons

If you eat something outrageous and don't take a photo for Instagram, did you really eat it? These restaurants feature dishes that are Instagram famous. These foods must be seen (and snapped) to be believed, and luckily they taste as good as they look!

Cheers to a fabulous night out in Philly! These spots add a little glam to your grub and are perfect for marking a special occasion.

Follow this icon when you're crawling for local brews and cocktails. This symbol points out the establishments that are best known for their great drinks. The food never fails here, but be sure to come thirsty too!

This icon means that sweet treats are ahead. Bring your sweet tooth to these spots for dessert first (or second or third)!

Philadelphia is for brunch. Look for this icon when crawling with a crew that needs sweet and savory (or an excuse to drink before noon).

Philadelphia loves its meatless Mondays and meat-reduced options. Look for this icon when crawling with vegans and vegetarians in your crew.

THE CHESTNUT HILL CRAWL

1. BAKER STREET BREAD CO., **8009 Germantown Ave., Philadelphia, (267) 336-7410, bakerstreetbread.com**

2. BREDENBECK'S BAKERY & ICE CREAM PARLOR, **8126 Germantown Ave., Philadelphia, (215) 247-7374, bredenbecks.com**

3. CAKE, **8501 Germantown Ave., Philadelphia, (215) 247-6887, cakeofchestnuthill.com**

4. ZIPF'S CANDIES, **8433 Germantown Ave., Philadelphia, (215) 248-1877**

5. BARRY'S BUNS, **Market at the Fareway, 8221 Germantown Ave., Philadelphia, (267) 521-2867, barrysbuns.com**

6. CHESTNUT HILL BREWING COMPANY, **Market at the Fareway, 8221 Germantown Ave., Philadelphia, (215) 247-0300, chestnuthillbrewingcompany.com**

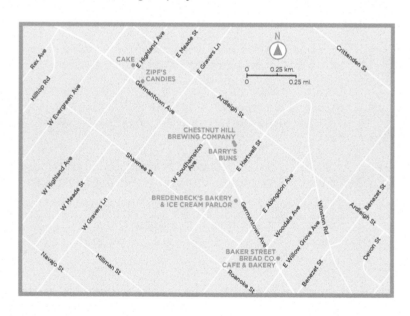

Chestnut Hill

Fancy neighborhood with down-to-earth eats

From the tree-lined streets to the stately Victorian mansions, Chestnut Hill, also referred to as the city's "Garden District" thanks to the Morris Arboretum and proximity to Fairmount Park, is one of Philly's most beautiful places to visit. From garden centers to antiques shops to taprooms and delicious restaurants, it's a great place to spend a day strolling through one of the most affluent areas of the city. A town lush with culture, education (Chestnut Hill College is right there), and recreation, Chestnut Hill is the perfect city escape without ever really leaving the city. Located just twenty-five minutes from Center City, trade the city subway for some good walking shoes and take a stroll down Germantown Avenue, trying some of the tastiest bites in the area.

1

BAKER STREET BREAD CO.

When you enter the sunny little storefront that is BAKER STREET BREAD CO., you may notice a few things. First, the literal wall of fresh-baked breads and baked goods. Second, the smell of fresh dough, bubbling away in the oven. And third, perhaps most importantly, the smiles of local patrons happily sipping coffee, enjoying a slow, delicious start to their day. That's about to be you, as you start your food tour of Chestnut Hill with breakfast at Baker Street.

Your meal should start with a house-made latte, paired with a slice of quiche and fresh fruit. The quiche features light and airy eggs in a buttery crust that melts in your mouth, and it's a dish that won't weigh you down.

BRAIDED CHALLAH

BAKER STREET BREAD C?
BRIOCHE BURGER
$1.00

BAKER STREET BREAD C?
MAPLE WALNUT SCONE

BAKER STREET BREAD C?
MULTI GRAIN DINNER

Then, try an acai bowl (if you've never had one, it's a smoothie bowl of blended acai, fruits, and more, typically served with various toppings). The Baker Street acai bowl is deliciously sweet, topped with granola and fresh fruit. Getting a bit heavier, try the breakfast burrito, which has fresh avocado and beans and is perfect for those who like their eggs handheld. If you like breakfast sandwiches, you're in luck, because Baker Street makes a breakfast sandwich with fluffy steamed eggs, tomato, avocado, and cheddar jack cheese (the Californian), and it's served on their amazing house-made bread. Lastly, to end things on a sweet note, try the French toast, which is also made with Baker Street Bread Co.'s house-made bread and is a perfect treat to wrap up your breakfast. The bread holds up beautifully against the sweet, sticky maple syrup, and a few pieces of fresh fruit are all that's needed to tie the dish together. However, don't wear out your sweet tooth just yet. . . .

2 BREDENBECK'S BAKERY & ICE CREAM PARLOR

The BREDENBECK'S story actually begins in 1889, when Frederick Robert Bredenbeck, an immigrant baker from Bavaria, opened up shop in Philadelphia's Northern Liberties neighborhood. The bakery was wildly successful and expanded into other parts of Philadelphia, including Mayfair and Germantown. The Bredenbeck family turned ownership over to two longtime employees, Walter and Otto Haug, in 1954. Fast-forward thirty years to 1983, and Walter's daughter, Karen H. Boyd-Rhode, opened Bredenbeck's Bakery & Ice Cream Parlor in Chestnut Hill.

Bredenbeck's is a true past-meets-present shop, where you can still get the time-honored traditional pastries that made Bredenbeck's famous, or you can get new, original, beautiful creations that are more modern. Nowadays, Bredenbeck's is heralded as one of the best places to get custom cakes, with a talented team of bakers and decorators (artists, really) at the ready. If you're just looking for some goodies to satisfy a sweet

tooth, they also have a great shop where you can ogle the pastry cases until something strikes your fancy. Try their strawberry shortcake, which was voted the best cake in Pennsylvania by *Business Insider*. It's light and fluffy, and the fresh strawberries add just the right amount of tanginess. You also must grab a cupcake from the case—they're all good, but strawberry champagne is a personal favorite. It's a light and fluffy vanilla cake topped with strawberry champagne buttercream—who says you can't eat your cocktail? If you have kids with you (or whimsical adults), the unicorn frosted cookie is a year-round hit. Bredenbeck's is known for their artistry with their baked goods, and the unicorn cookie is no exception—each one is hand-decorated with bright, colorful frosting that is as tasty as it is pretty. Lastly, you cannot leave Bredenbeck's without trying some of their pound cake. They have a few flavors, but chocolate chip is particularly delicious. It's dense, moist, dotted with tiny chocolate chips, and then covered in a thick smattering of frosting. It's quintessentially Philly and quintessentially Bredenbeck's. Now that your sweet tooth has been satisfied (don't worry if it's not; there's more in store), get ready for a gorgeous brunch in an even-more-gorgeous setting!

3 CAKE

Ever eaten in an old greenhouse? No? Well, you're in luck. **CAKE** is a restaurant where the space is as pretty as the food. Upon walking in, your jaw will drop—a giant fountain in the center of the restaurant, vines crawling up the walls, and an abundance of natural light throughout the all-glass building. This is the spot in Chestnut Hill to grab lunch or brunch, depending on the day you come. On Sunday they serve a brunch menu only, whereas you can get breakfast/lunch Tuesday through Saturday (they're closed on

Monday). If you make it for lunch, try a sandwich or a burger, both of which are guaranteed to fill you up. However, if you're lucky enough to snag a table during Sunday brunch (no reservations), you're in for a real treat.

Start your meal off with the baked brie, which comes with port wine–poached figs and a warm baguette. The crispy bread is the perfect vehicle for the creamy, gooey cheese, and the poached figs are sweet and just a bit tart, which cuts through the richness of the cheese. For your main event, the Norwegian-Style Smoked Salmon is excellent. Thinly sliced smoked salmon is topped with a green salad, upon which rests a giant dill potato latke, dressed up with horseradish crème fraîche and a dollop of caviar. It's the super-indulgent brunch dish you didn't know you needed. Lastly, if you're not sick of sweets yet (which, let's be honest, you can't be), grab a tart from their pastry case, which is full of beautiful pastry creations that you can enjoy in-house or take to go. Hopefully you haven't exhausted your sweet tooth yet, because we're about to take a step back in time at our next stop.

4

ZIPF'S CANDIES

Chocolates that look like olives? Hot wine-flavored candy? Spun molasses chocolates? You can find all that and more at ZIPF'S. Zipf's has been a Chestnut Hill staple since 1968, carrying candies and chocolates from around the world. This is the place to come for candy that you really won't find anywhere else, and upon walking in you'll quite literally have one of those "kid in a candy store" freak-outs because of the sheer amount of beautifully wrapped candies that adorn the little shop. From a display case full of gorgeous chocolates to the boxes of marzipan and maple candy, there's something for every sweet tooth at Zipf's. What makes them so special is that they carry retro candy that is nearly impossible to get elsewhere, as well as an array of imported candies from all over the world. People

come in just to get their assorted licorice (of which there is no shortage). Licorices are imported from Europe and come in every variety, from soft to chewy to sweet to salted (yes, salted licorice is quite popular!). Grab yourself a few interesting candies to go as you make your way to the next sweet spot.

5

BARRY'S BUNS

What business does a guy named Joel Singer have running a bakery called **BARRY'S BUNS**? Well, first off, Barry is his middle name. Second, he's a seasoned pastry chef with over twenty years of experience and an extensive culinary résumé (like creating fantastic baked goods at the Pennsylvania Convention Center and The Rittenhouse Hotel). Joel always dreamed of having his own bakery, and sticky buns were his beloved childhood dessert, so with wife Jen by his side to run the business side of things, Barry's Buns opened in the Market at the Fareway in Chestnut Hill in 2016. Nowadays, every Thursday through Saturday people flock to

the bakery to pick up Joel's innovative buns, cupcakes, cakes, and more.

The first thing you'll notice at Barry's is that everything looks and smells amazing. Spoiler alert: It all tastes incredible too. This is not the place to stick to whatever diet you're on—trust me, you're going to want to indulge. Kick things off with some crumb cake, which is a textural marvel. The cake is super-moist and dense, while the topping is crunchy and much thicker than what you're used to on a run-of-the-mill crumb cake. Next, ease into the sugar coma with a cupcake, which is baked without any shortening or shortcuts—real butter, real sugar, real flavor. Red velvet is particularly delicious, as the chocolatey cake pairs beautifully with the tangy cream-cheese frosting. Now, for the big guns. Get some assorted buns—yes, multiple. Barry's cranks out a ton of innovative flavors and is constantly coming up with new creations to please the palate. From classics like walnut, apple crumb, and cream-cheese frosted to seasonal flavors like German chocolate (with coconut, pecans, and dark chocolate), Barry's takes great pride in their ability to sling an outrageous quantity of buns while still maintaining high quality. Lastly, you must try the giant sticky bun. The bun is roughly the size of your hand, and the entire bun is frosted. The best way to tackle it is to just bite right in and be delighted as flavors of cinnamon, brown sugar, and cream-cheese frosting dance on your tongue. Now, in case you're in a full-on sugar coma, you're in luck, because the final stop of this food tour is just a few steps away (and involves a salad).

TIP

Barry's has a second location in The Bourse Food Hall in Old City, so you can get their tasty creations there as well!

6 CHESTNUT HILL BREWING COMPANY

CHESTNUT HILL BREWING COMPANY (CHBC) is the perfect place to end your food crawl for two reasons: good food and good beer. In addition to a full food menu, CHBC brews and sells delicious, small-batch craft beer made on-site in their 5BBL system. They pride themselves in producing a variety of well-balanced beers, from pilsners to IPAs to stouts, so there is really something for everyone.

Once you choose a brew, it's time for some eats. What goes great with beer? Pizza, of course. So try one of CHBC's house-made pizzas. The Margherita is a classic, and the Trenton is a classic flipped upside down (literally). On the Trenton pie the sauce is on the top and the cheese is on the bottom, which totally changes the experience (in a good way). Since

TIP

CHBC doesn't distribute
their beer, but you can grab
a Crowler or Growler to go!

you're probably feeling pretty full,
you may be craving something
light. If that's the case, the Firepit
Salad is an excellent choice. This
salad starts with an arugula and
red leaf base, and it's topped with
roasted corn, roasted red pepper, pickled red onion, avocado,
cocoa sunflower weeds, queso
fresco, and is dressed in a smoked
chili vinaigrette. While it may be
a lighter option, this salad is not
light on flavor, combining sweet,
smoky, tangy, and creamy flavor in
every bite.

Now, just because the Chestnut
Hill food tour is over doesn't mean
the fun is. Grab a seat at the bar,
try some brews, and have a great
night!

BONUS CRAWL! VEGAN EATS

1. **DOTTIE'S DONUTS**, 509 S. 6th St., Philadelphia, (267) 761-9447

2. **DIZENGOFF**, 1625 Sansom St., Philadelphia, (215) 867-8181, dizengoffhummus.com

3. **20TH STREET PIZZA**, 108 S. 20th St., Philadelphia, (215) 398-5748, 20thstreet.pizza

4. **HIPCITYVEG**, 127 S. 18th St., Philadelphia, (215) 278-7605, hipcityveg.com

5. **BAR BOMBÓN**, 133 S. 18th St., Philadelphia, (267) 606-6612, barbombon.com

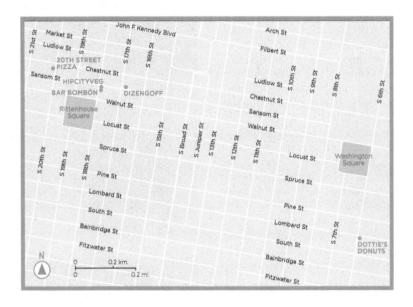

Bonus Crawl! Vegan Eats

When people hear "plant-based," they often shirk away, thinking that breakfast, lunch, and dinner will be a big bowl of raw vegetables. No dairy? No meat? No animal products at all? The horror! However, Philly is a city that completely flips the script, with restaurants cranking out plant-based meals that are so good, you'd never know they're vegan. It's environmentally friendly and an all-around healthier alternative that you can feel good about—so get ready to have your mind blown as we crawl through Chestnut Hill's best vegan eats.

1 DOTTIE'S DONUTS

What would you eat for breakfast if calories didn't matter? For this blogger, it's donuts for sure. However, if you're looking for a vegan donut, your options are pretty limited. At least they were until **DOTTIE'S DONUTS** took the Philly dessert scene by storm, making plant-based donuts that are both delicious and Insta-worthy. Dottie's started as a wholesale operation, stocking local bakeries and cafes with their vegan treats, before opening their first shop in West Philly. They've since opened a second location in Queen Village, which you'll be visiting for the tastiest vegan breakfast you can imagine—a bunch of awesome baked goods.

Start off with an apple fritter, which is literally the size of your face. It's light and fluffy, bursting with apple flavor, and covered in a thin layer

of decadent glaze. It's as good as any apple fritter you've ever had but is completely devoid of animal products. Next, treat yourself to a donut (or two or three). The flavors rotate regularly, so try whatever is in season! Dottie's staff is always happy to make recommendations as well. Pictured is the cranberry vanilla donut, which is tart and fruity but balanced nicely by the sweet vanilla drizzle. Now, use all of that donut-fueled energy to start the trek to the next stop, as your vegan feast through Philly kicks off.

Famous Vegans

Did you know that some of your favorite celebrities are vegan?

Zac Efron, Beyoncé, Natalie Portman, Madonna, Venus Williams, Miley Cyrus, and Joaquin Phoenix are just some of Hollywood's most famous plant-based celebs.

2 DIZENGOFF

Hummus tends to be a staple in vegan diets, since it's readily available at grocery stores and restaurants and can easily be made vegan. However, store-bought hummus is boring and the same old roasted garlic hummus on rotation can get old. Meet DIZENGOFF, a hummus-lovers paradise. Modeled after the stands found throughout Israel, Dizengoff serves freshly made hummus with a rotating variety of toppings. While not 100 percent vegan, Dizengoff has a number of vegan options that make for a killer meal.

It is first worth noting that the pita bread at Dizengoff is legendary. Soft and pillowy, yet thick and sturdy enough to pile on the hummus and all the toppings your heart desires (and trust me—here, you're bound to desire some toppings). The menu isn't huge—you have your base of hummus and then you can choose meat or veggie toppings. If you stick with the veggie options, then you can easily keep it vegan. The toppings change throughout the year, so check the board when

TIP

Every Sunday starting at 11, you can get shakshuka at Dizengoff, a fabulous North African dish of baked eggs in a spicy tomato-and-pepper stew, served with warm za'atar pita.

you walk in, or ask a friendly staff member for a suggestion. Pictured here are hummus topped with asparagus, olive oil, and pine nuts; hummus topped with assorted pickled vegetables; and hummus topped with olive oil and crispy chickpeas. Which one's the best? Well, that's like asking to pick your favorite child. The asparagus hummus is perfectly light, and the flavors of the pine nuts and olive oil complement the asparagus beautifully. The pickled vegetable hummus is an excellent mix of creamy hummus and tart, pickled vegetables that are perfectly crunchy. The chickpea hummus is crunchy, spiced, and so good it'll leave you licking the plate. Every hummus also comes with a side of little pickles and a chopped salad, both of which are vegan and extremely tasty—the perfect bite to cut through the thick, creamy tehina hummus that's made Dizengoff so famous. Once you've had your fill of hummus, get ready to load up on some pizza that's so delicious, you'd never know it was vegan.

3

20TH STREET PIZZA

Mark Mebus is no stranger to kick-ass vegan food. He owns a number of pizzerias throughout the city (Blackbird Pizzeria is extremely well known in the city and worth a stop if you're nearby), but wanted to open a restaurant where he was putting forth the best pizza that he could produce without compromise. While 20TH STREET PIZZA may be a casual establishment, it's laser-focused on quality.

If you've ever eaten pizza in your life (if you haven't, there's a whole crawl for that), you know that it all starts with good dough, and 20th Street Pizza takes great pride in their dough. They mill their own spelt, everything is naturally leavened (no commercial yeast is used), and there's a long, slow fermentation process to get the perfect dough that is the base of their pizzas. Next: toppings. 20th Street's toppings are mostly organic and local, and heavily vegetable focused.

Now, what to order here? They sell by the slice, which is perfect for trying out a few things. They used to exclusively do square pies but have now begun doing traditional pies as well, so you can get a great mix. The plain square pie, topped with tomato sauce, a shredded vegan cheese blend, and basil, is a delicious, classic slice. The white pizza features a cashew ricotta that's made in-house with a vegan cheese blend, garlic, parsley, and olive oil for a simple, tomato-free pizza experience. The Balboa, an homage to one of Philly's idols, is topped with arugula, "sausage" (which is made of mushroom and seitan), cashew ricotta, pistachio pesto, and tomato sauce for a wonderful blend of cheesy, meaty goodness, without

any cheese or meat. The Hand of Shroom slice is perfect for mushroom lovers, topped with roasted mushrooms, vinegar-roasted red onions, vegan cheese blend, and a garlic cream sauce. Lastly, the Hot Potato slice is topped with thinly sliced potato, smoked onions, and a spicy pistachio pesto that gives just the right amount of heat. Bonus: 20th Street Pizza is also certified Kosher in addition to being 100 percent vegan!

4 HIPCITYVEG

How many times have you already said "Wow, I can't believe this is vegan" on this crawl? Get ready to say it again, as HIPCITYVEG specializes in creating vegan versions of your favorite fast food, from burgers to chicken nuggets. Nicole Marquis opened up HipCityVeg in 2012 with the goal of bringing people delicious, plant-based food in a form they already loved: fast food. The menu is familiar and enticing, but everything is completely vegan, made with sustainability in mind. Using only 100 percent organic non-GMO soy, HipCityVeg is able to offer a product that's both better and better for you than your typical fast food (vegan or not).

Kick off your meal with some sweet potato fries, which are the perfect vehicle for the insanely delicious house sauce. Dubbed HipCityVeg Sauce, this magical sauce is a mystical combination of sweet and spicy goodness that pairs perfectly with the sweet, crispy fries. Next, try a burger—particularly, the Smokehouse Burger, which is a Beyond Meat patty loaded with crispy onions, tangy BBQ sauce, and smoked Gouda cheese. It's as good as any burger you've had, but it's a choice you can feel good about! Lastly, you must try a Chick'n sandwich. I'm not entirely sure what voodoo they're doing in the kitchen to create a plant-based substitute that looks, tastes, smells, and feels like chicken, but we should all be thankful, because the Chick'n sandwiches are outrageously good. The Crispy HipCity Ranch sandwich has a battered Chick'n patty, lettuce, tomato, pickles, and peppercorn ranch—it's really a perfect riff on a fast-food classic. Now, it's time to wash all of this vegan goodness down with some drinks and bites at our final stop.

5 BAR BOMBÓN

The last stop of this plant-based food tour lands you at BAR BOMBÓN, a Latin American restaurant known for their vegan spin on everything from tacos to empanadas.

The first thing you'll notice is the dark, sultry vibe of the restaurant (hello, date night!). It's a small spot,

but you also have the option of sitting at the bar. Next, you'll notice that everything coming out of the kitchen looks, well, not vegan. That's pretty standard of owner Nicole Marquis—making vegan food that doesn't look, feel, or taste vegan, which is what makes this spot so interesting.

Start your meal with Philly Steak Empanadas, which are an ode to Philadelphia. They come in a crunchy, well-seasoned outer shell, filled with vegan meat and cheese, served with a side of spicy ketchup. Next, the Peruvian Yucca is a delightful, light starter, served with an aji amarillo sauce, Castelvetrano olives, fried capers, and a dash of cilantro for a mix of earthy, salty, sweet, creamy, and tart all in one bite. The last starter should be guacamole, and if there's a

seasonal special, try that out. Pictured is the guacamole with pineapple and pomegranate, served with crispy veggie chips. For some heartier plates, you must try their tacos and sliders, which are some of the restaurant's most beloved dishes. The Buffalo Cauliflower Tacos are crispy, spicy, and perfectly balanced by the beans, avocado, and cilantro dressing inside of them. The Cubano Club Slider features blackened Chick'n (yes, the same kind you can get at Marquis's other restaurant, HipCityVeg), smoked tempeh, avocado, pickles, lettuce, and a grain mustard aioli. It's guaranteed to make you, yet again, go "Wow, I can't believe this is vegan!"

THE CHINATOWN CRAWL

1. A LA MOUSSE, **145 N. 11th St., Philadelphia, (215) 238-9100**

2. DIM SUM GARDEN, **1020 Race St., Philadelphia, (215) 873-0258, dimsumgardenphilly.com**

3. TERAKAWA RAMEN, **204 N. 9th St., Philadelphia, (267) 687-1355, terakawaramen.com**

4. YAMITSUKI, **1028 Arch St. #19107, Philadelphia, (215) 629-3888, yamitsukiramen.com**

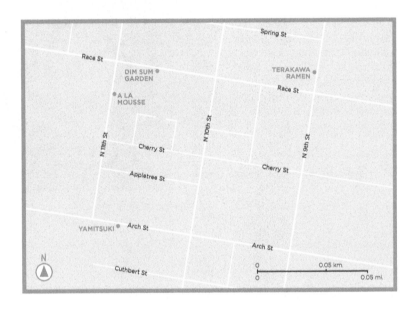

Chinatown

All that and dim sum

Get ready to get immersed into Philadelphia's vibrant Asian neighborhood, affectionately referred to by locals as Chinatown. Denoted by the beautiful Chinatown Friendship Gate at the intersection of 10th and Arch Streets, this area was initially settled by Cantonese immigrants in the mid-1900s. Chinatown is an area bustling with fantastic food and an abundance of things to see and do. The neighborhood is packed with restaurants and stores representing everything from Taiwanese culture to Korean, Thai, Malaysian, Chinese, and everything in between.

1

A LA MOUSSE

We're starting this food crawl on a sweet note, at this cozy cafe that specializes in matcha-forward desserts. Everything at A LA MOUSSE is made in-house, and they make a point to put out desserts that aren't tooth-hurtingly sweet (hence, it's totally fine to have dessert for breakfast). They also serve coffee, espresso, and various teas (including milk teas) to pair with your sweet morning bites.

The best way to decide what to get here is really just to check out the pastry case and see what appeals to you. The lychee panna cotta is a fan favorite, with light notes of lychee fruit and a creamy texture. If you like lychee, try the lychee rose mousse, which has an airy texture and a pleasant floral taste. The tangerine cake is also a fun treat, which is served to look like a real tangerine, leaf and all. It's tangy and bright and pairs well with a tea. You should also try one of their matcha desserts, since that's their specialty. The Matcha Cake is light and melts in your mouth, with delightful hints of matcha that aren't overpowering or bitter.

Once you've finished enjoying your morning treats, get ready to experience some of Chinatown's best cuisine.

2 DIM SUM GARDEN

The story of DIM SUM GARDEN begins in 2003, when head chef Shizhou Da came to the United States with an original recipe for xiao long bao (Chinese steamed soup dumplings). A fifth generation removed from the chef who originally pioneered xiao long bao in China, Da used her thirty-plus years of experience in making fresh, traditional-style dim sum to bring Shanghai's beloved dumplings to Philadelphia in 2013.

> **TIP**
>
> This place has historically been BYOB but now serves beer and wine. You can still bring your own for a $15 corkage fee. For these reasons, this place is a favorite for group outings.

It goes without saying that you must order the Shanghai steamed pork soup dumplings. They're soft and tender, bursting with warm soup, with a flavorful meat core. The pan-fried beef dumplings should be your next choice. Hearty and bursting with flavor, these dumplings are steamed and then quickly pan fried, giving them a crispy outer shell that makes for an excellent mouthfeel. Lastly, mix things up with the Shanghai Shao Mai, which comes with four large pieces and are extremely hearty for a dumpling. They have a soft texture and pleasant, mild flavor profile that serves as a great contrast to the other items.

As you wrap up your dim sum experience, get excited, because now it's ramen time.

3 TERAKAWA RAMEN

Many people will argue that TERAKAWA RAMEN has the best ramen in Philadelphia (and they might be right). This shop serves authentic, handmade Japanese ramen, with the chef's recipes originating from the Kumamoto region of Japan. Their broth simmers for two days and their noodles are all handmade, so this place is not messing around.

The menu features a number of Japanese appetizers, curry platters, donburi (rice bowl dishes), and ramen, which is what you're here for. Go right for the Terakawa Ramen, which is their signature creation. The pork broth is made from Natural Heritage Berkshire Pork Bones, and the bowl is topped with char siu (roast pork). Inside the ramen you'll also find bamboo

shoots, kikurage mushrooms, red ginger, chopped scallions, and a perfectly seasoned soft-boiled egg. While it will be tempting to start loading it up with all of the sauces and seasonings you can, resist the urge and let yourself enjoy the full experience properly. First, taste the broth. Second, taste the noodles, which are straighter, lighter-colored noodles that differ from the traditional egg noodles typically found in ramen. Next, take in the different textures of the ramen—the soft egg, the al dente noodles, the crunchy veggies and tender pork. Then, flavor the broth and noodles using the spices at your table and allow your entire dish to evolve in flavor with each bite.

Finish slurping up your ramen and get ready for more delicious Asian fare at our next stop!

4 YAMITSUKI

YAMITSUKI is another spot serving up crazy-good ramen with a full Asian-fusion menu. In addition to ramen, you can get sushi, crudo, steamed buns, teas—you name it, you can likely get it here. It also carries a selection of Japanese beer and sake, so it's a great place to expand your palate and your drinking horizons.

You should definitely start your meal off with a specialty roll, as the chef prides himself in sourcing the highest-quality product. If you like eel, the Fancy Dragon Roll is delicious. It's filled with shrimp tempura and topped with smoked salmon, eel, eel sauce, and spicy mayo, for a true umami sensation. Next, try some sashimi—preferably the chef's sampler, in which you can get six pieces of the chef's choice of sashimi. Lastly, this is another spot known for rockin' ramen, so try one of them. They make a variety of broths, but the Tonkotsu ramen is the one to go for. Tonkotsu ramen has a silky, almost buttery pork broth with sea salt for a salty yet almost creamy mouthfeel. The dish also features noodles, seaweed, a soft-boiled egg,

fish cake, and your choice of meat (I recommend pork). It's a unique flavor combination that perfectly contrasts with the previous spot to show that just because two places make similar dishes doesn't mean they're the same.

BONUS CRAWL! CAFE CRAWL

1. **LA COLOMBE COFFEE ROASTERS** (multiple locations), 1335 Frankford Ave., Philadelphia, (267) 479-1600, lacolombe.com

2. **REANIMATOR COFFEE** (multiple locations), 1523 E. Susquehanna Ave., Philadelphia, (215) 425-5805, reanimatorcoffee.com

3. **MENAGERIE COFFEE**, 18 S. 3rd St., Philadelphia, menageriecoffee.com

4. **ELIXR COFFEE ROASTERS** (multiple locations), 207 S. Sydenham St., Philadelphia, elixrcoffee.com

5. **VIBRANT COFFEE ROASTERS**, 222 W. Rittenhouse Square, 1st Floor, Philadelphia, (267) 225-4240, vibrantcoffeeroasters.com

6. **K'FAR CAFE**, 110 S. 19th St., Philadelphia, (267) 800-7200, kfarcafe.com

7. **VERNICK COFFEE BAR** (inside Comcast Technology Center), 1 N. 19th St., Philadelphia, (215) 419-5052, vernickcoffeebar.com

8. **RIVAL BROS. COFFEE BAR**, 1100 Tasker St., Philadelphia, (877) 585-1085, rivalbros.com

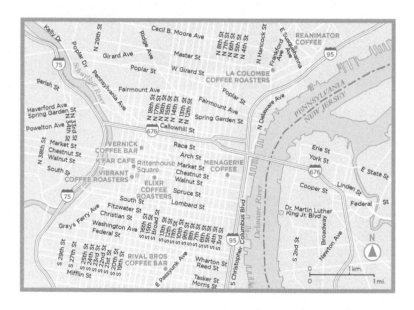

Bonus Crawl! Cafe Crawl

While New York is "The City That Never Sleeps," Philly is the city that "sleeps sometimes but has a lot of stuff to get done today, and a nap just isn't in the cards so pass the coffee." While Philly takes food seriously, it seriously does not mess around when it comes to good coffee. From the tiny independent shops sprinkled throughout the city to the local roasters shipping nationwide, there is no shortage of good java in Philadelphia. The cafes in Philly's various neighborhoods serve more than just a good cup of coffee—many of them offer a community gathering space, mouthwatering bites, and one-of-a-kind atmospheres that make you want to get your cup of joe "for here." One of the coolest ways to see Philadelphia can actually be by hopping from one cafe to the next, moving from North, to Central, to South Philadelphia, one delicious sip at a time.

1   LA COLOMBE COFFEE ROASTERS

A nationwide cafe chain with humble roots in Philadelphia, you can now find LA COLOMBE cafes from NYC to Boston to California. You can easily identify a La Colombe cafe by its cool, industrial vibe and unmistakable smell of a fresh, bold roast brewing. La Colombe really has something for everyone—if you like your coffee bold and dark or if you're more of a latte type, there's an array of delicious brews (and tasty bites to go with them) to ensure that nobody has to go uncaffeinated.

For something classic, try a latte. The La Colombe baristas are notorious for making even the simplest coffee drinks look beautiful (hello, latte art!). Pair that with a pastry and you've got the breakfast (or snack) of champions. For something uniquely La Colombe, try their draft lattes. They pioneered the concept of draft lattes to create a true latte experience in a cold, to-go form. To achieve the perfect cold latte that you can take anywhere, founders JP Iberti and Todd Carmichael created a cold brew concentrate and mixed it with nitrous and milk so that every can is as luscious and satisfying as an in-cafe drink. If you're looking for what's popular, pure black cold brew is their top seller. At the cafes you can get it topped with a bit of draft latte, which creates a truly unique coffee experience.

Every La Colombe coffee shop (there are four in Philadelphia) prides itself on being a true gathering space for locals and out-of-towners alike. None of the cafes have Wi-Fi, and all of them have communal counter seating in addition to tables, encouraging people to stay a while, chat, and connect with their peers. La Colombe is creating more than great coffee—they're creating a community.

One of the best things about La Colombe is that when you leave the shop, you can take their delicious coffee with you (or find it at retailers and restaurants across the city). Any store/restaurant brewing La Colombe has been trained by La Colombe baristas, ensuring that you get the same experience across any location. You can find draft lattes and bags of coffee beans for sale in each of their locations, and they sell an assortment of flavors and roasts that are super-unique.

2 REANIMATOR COFFEE

If you're looking for some rich, strong, kick-in-the-ass coffee that will literally bring you back to life, then you need some REANIMATOR. Heralded as one of Philly's beloved roasteries, ReAnimator is focused on more than just unique beans and complex roasts, they're focused on the coffee experience.

From the first time you walk into a ReAnimator shop, you're hit with the intoxicating aromas of fresh roasting coffee as you take in the cool, airy vibes and diverse clientele. Grab something espresso-based—whether that be a latte, cappuccino, or straight shot, it's sure to give you the jolt you need with the rich taste you desire.

While you're there, strike up a conversation with a barista. ReAnimator prides themselves in proliferating coffee knowledge, whether about the roasting, blending, or drink-crafting process.

HOW DO YOU LIKE YOUR COFFEE?

Espresso: 1 ounce of highly concentrated coffee

Red Eye: 1 shot of espresso + 6 ounces drip brewed coffee

Americano: 1 shot of espresso + 3 ounces hot water

Cortado: 1 shot of espresso + 1 ounce warm milk + 1 cm foam

Cappuccino: espresso + 2 ounces steamed milk + 2 ounces foamed milk

Cafe Latte: 1 shot of espresso + 8 to 10 ounces steamed milk + 1 cm foam

Cafe au Lait: 5 ounces French press coffee + 5 ounces scalded milk

3

MENAGERIE COFFEE

When Elysa and April moved to Philadelphia from Madison, Wisconsin, they brought with them a love for fine art, music, and hospitality. Both started working at various coffee shops in the city, and the need for a specialty cafe in Old City became abundantly clear. Thus, MENAGERIE was born.

Menagerie is part coffee shop, part neighborhood gathering space. From the artsy vibe to the bustling, diverse clientele, Menagerie is a truly inclusive space where all are welcome, and that's not just limited to the guests. When it comes to hiring baristas, this cafe cares so much about the client experience that they'll hire friendly applicants with little to no coffee experience, seeking to break down the barista stereotype.

Part of the charm of Menagerie is the simple menu made from quality ingredients that pairs perfectly with their robust coffee offerings. From a simple latte to a cortado (all of which you can get with a wide variety of dairy and nondairy milks), Menagerie uses coffee from Elixr (Philadelphia), Dogwood (Minneapolis, Minnesota), and Tandem Coffee (Portland, Maine) to create a truly satisfying, crafted coffee experience. They purposely source from various roasters, pulling unique flavor profiles into their different beverages.

If you're looking for a bite to pair with your coffee, their breakfast sandwich is a perfectly balanced, simple accompaniment to any drink. The sandwich features egg, ham, pepper jack, and maple syrup on a pressed English muffin. It's sweet, salty, cheesy, and utterly satisfying. Be sure to finish your visit off with a house-made cookie—they're chewy, soft, and a great way to end a delicious visit.

4 ELIXR COFFEE ROASTERS

Light-roast-coffee lovers rejoice—finally a cafe that prides itself in flavorful, lighter roasts that all can enjoy. Don't get me wrong—I love a cup of extra-dark jet fuel as much as the next person, but sometimes I just want a flavorful coffee that won't make my eyeballs vibrate. ELIXR was founded in 2010 by Evan Inatome, with the mission of perfecting the sourcing, roasting, and preparation of coffee in the greater Philadelphia area and beyond. Did you know that coffee competitions

were a thing? Because Elixr has won just about all of them—from National Barista competitions to Best Cold Brew in America—they know coffee.

If you're visiting Elixr's Center City location, expect: A. a witty sign outside as well as a super-chic mural that's begging to be in your Instagram story; B. a modern industrial vibe in the cafe that invites you to stay a while; and C. damn good coffee.

The menu isn't huge and you can find all of the standard variations of caffeinated beverages that you normally would, but Elixr has some killer seasonal specials that are definitely worth branching out. Pictured here is the Lavender Cardamom latte, which has a delicate light roast that perfectly pairs with the floral notes of the lavender and cardamom. Grab some Philly-local baked goods and a seat, and enjoy

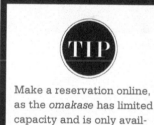

TIP

Make a reservation online, as the *omakase* has limited capacity and is only available on weekends.

your little cup of heaven right in the center of Philadelphia.

For a super-special coffee experience, you can also hit up Elixr's coffee *omakase* (Japanese phrase that means "I'll leave it up to you"), where on weekends you can try six different variations/preparations of coffee in a chef's tasting style.

5

VIBRANT COFFEE ROASTERS

Sister company to Function Coffee Labs, Vibrant knows coffee (and knows it well). Right off Rittenhouse Square, the tiny shop would be easy to miss if it weren't for the bright (dare I say, vibrant) sign. The shop and menu are small, but both pack a mighty punch.

To drink, grab a seasonal latte, which is always inventive and delicious. In the summer, a Cinnamon Toast Crunch Latte is sure to make you feel like a kid again—reminiscent of sipping the cinnamon-infused milk after a tasty breakfast. In the winter, a Gingerbread or Spicy Orange latte are the perfect winter warmer, with layers of spice. If you're feeling peckish, the folks at Vibrant are sourdough experts, making incredible sourdough breads and baked goods. For a savory bite, their avocado toast is simple

and excellent—flavorful, filling, and made better by insanely good bread. For something sweet, a salted rye chocolate chip cookie or seasonal scone might tickle your fancy. However, you cannot (I repeat, *cannot*) leave Vibrant Coffee Roasters without trying a Cruffin. A croissant-muffin hybrid, this delectable treat is also filled with flavored pastry cream and topped with toasted meringue. The flavors change regularly but are always incredible and pair great with a tasty coffee!

6

K'FAR CAFE

The brainchild of the brilliant team behind Zahav (one of the nation's top restaurants, right here in Philly), Abe Fisher, Federal Donuts, Goldie Falafel, Dizengoff, and more, it's no surprise that K'FAR CAFE is a slam dunk.

First things first, the aesthetic of the cafe is unmatched. Between the marble counters, rose gold accents, and hints of pink, it's a millennial paradise that's both charming and modern at once. The cafe specializes in Israeli cuisine, baked goods, and java. Upon arriving you're likely to immediately take note of the pastry case, which is stocked with rugelach, chocolate babka, pistachio sticky buns, and tehina chocolate chip cookies. You should get all of these things. Next, you'll notice that they don't serve just any old bagels—they serve Jerusalem bagels, which are oblong, seed-covered, and delightfully crisp. Try the smoked salmon bagel, which is smoky, tangy, and refreshing all at once. If you're looking for more substance, the Tunisian Salad with tuna, egg, potato, olive, and preserved lemon is extremely well executed.

What pairs better with baked goods than amazing coffee? You must try a Yemenite latte, which you won't find anywhere else. This latte has cardamom, ginger, and cinnamon, expertly blended for a drink that is sweet, floral, tangy, and delicious. If that's not your jam, you can't go

wrong with any of their coffees—a latte with almond milk is my go-to, as it is neutral enough to pair with the chocolate babka and three rugelach that I'm inevitably eating.

TIP

Beat the crowds here by coming off-hours (before 11:30 a.m. or after 2 p.m.).

7 VERNICK COFFEE BAR

VERNICK COFFEE BAR is a joint venture between James Beard Award–winning Chef Greg Vernick and the Four Seasons at the New Comcast Technology Center (which is a spectacle to behold in itself). Greg Vernick is well known for his namesake restaurant, Vernick Food & Drink, which is frequently heralded as one of Philly's best. The idea behind the coffee bar was to bring Chef Vernick's global flavors into a more casual environment so that Philadelphians and tourists alike could experience it. The coffee bar itself has a forty-seat full-service restaurant that operates for breakfast and lunch, and it is an absolute must-visit for coffee lovers.

Vernick Coffee Bar brews an extensive menu of coffees, teas, and fresh-pressed juices and is the only place in Philadelphia currently serving Umbria coffee, a Seattle-based roaster known for their worldly blends. Their standard lattes are bursting with flavor due to the fantastic coffee they start with, and expert baristas are as well versed in drink-making as they are latte art, so expect a pretty cup (Instagrammable). Pair your latte with one of their house-made pastries, all of which are available for takeaway (and trust me, you'll want some to go). Their carrot cake pie is a unique twist on a classic—a moist, zesty carrot cake fills a buttery pie shell and is topped with house-made cream-cheese frosting for a perfectly balanced bite. If you're after something fruity, the apple confit tart is a home run—buttery flaky crust; sweet, fresh apples; and a hint of gold leaf—because, why not?

Feeling adventurous? How about a Butterfly Pea Flower Matcha? This striking drink is bright blue topped with dark-green matcha, which makes for a seriously cool (and seriously tasty) beverage. Should you be seeking a more substantial pairing with your drink, you must try one of Vernick Coffee Bar's toasts. The English pea hummus toast is topped with tomatoes and a tahini vinaigrette, making for a fresh (and veggie-filled)

bite! If you're looking for a sweet-and-salty blend, then look no further than the Fromage Blanc toast, topped with figs and spiced honey. Each bite has a perfect blend of sweet yet spicy honey, delicate figs, creamy cheese, and hearty bread.

What's great about Vernick Coffee Bar is that it goes beyond the standard cafe—it's a true hybrid that's reflective of the on-the-go nature of Philadelphians, but still provides delicious cuisine and quality drinks.

8 RIVAL BROS. COFFEE BAR

Rival Bros. coffee is a perfect example of what happens when a chef (Jonathan Adams) and a roaster (Damien Pileggi) unite to create a truly memorable coffee experience.

Priding themselves in single-origin, responsibly sourced beans and unique blends, Rival Bros. coffee can now be found all around Philadelphia, and their cafes are a must-stop on the Philly cafe crawl.

While Rival Bros. has three shops in Philadelphia, the South Philly location is the newest, and it's situated right in the heart of the popular Passyunk neighborhood (a local favorite and must-visit for tourists and foodies). The shop is a blend of industrial and modern, with a

welcoming atmosphere, friendly baristas, and, of course, the heavenly scents of delicious coffee brewing. Try an oat milk latte, which is the perfect blend of bitter coffee and mellow oat milk but tastes different than a traditional latte. Pair that latte with one of their available pastries. Pictured is the chai Kouign Amann with espresso ganache, which is sweet, spiced, rich, and light and fluffy all at once. They also have a number of savory pastries (such as a Kale Spinach Gouda Bun) if you want something a bit more hearty.

On your way out, grab some ground or whole-bean coffee to enjoy the unique blends and roasts of the Rival Bros. at home.

THE FAIRMOUNT/MUSEUM DISTRICT CRAWL

1. STOCKYARD SANDWICH CO., **1541 Spring Garden St., Philadelphia, (215) 977-9273, stockyardphilly.com**

2. RYBREAD, **1711 Fairmount Ave., Philadelphia, (215) 769-0603, rybreadcafe.com**

3. TELA'S MARKET & KITCHEN, **1833 Fairmount Ave., Philadelphia, (215) 235-0170, telasmarket.com**

4. PIZZERIA VETRI, **1939 Callowhill St., Philadelphia, (215) 600-2629, pizzeriavetri.com**

5. A MANO, **2244 Fairmount Ave., Philadelphia, (215) 236-1114, amanophl.com**

6. UMAI UMAI, **533 N. 22nd St., Philadelphia, (215) 988-0707, umai-umai.com**

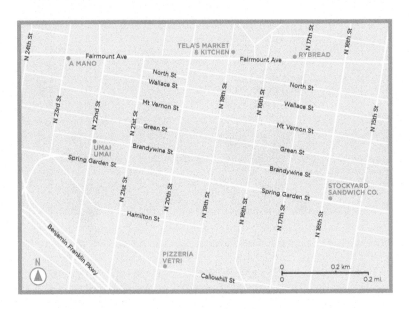

Fairmount/Museum District

Often referred to as the "Art Museum Area" due to its proximity to some of the city's (and nation's) most impressive collections of art, the Fairmount Neighborhood appeals to more than just art lovers. Bustling with families, foodies, and culture lovers alike, Fairmount is a piece of the city that feels more like a quiet suburb. With abundant greenery, it's a perfect area for an afternoon stroll. Amid the trees and parks, you'll find charming local shops, cafes, and delicious eateries that make Fairmount a can't-miss neighborhood on any Philadelphia visit.

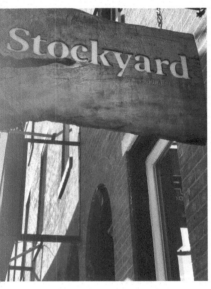

1 STOCKYARD SANDWICH CO.

What do you get when two alums of some of Philly's hottest restaurants get drunk together on a random night? You get one of Philly's best sandwich shops—STOCKYARD. This small storefront brings big flavor as owners Will Lindsay and Mike Metzger craft locally sourced nose-to-tail goodness.

If you're lucky enough to make it here on a weekend, you must try what was named one of Philly's best breakfast sandwiches. You can craft your own sandwich by picking your base (try the Everything Philly Muffin), your style of eggs, cheese, meat, and sauce. They butcher, cure, and season everything in-house, down to the bacon and breakfast sausage that graces their breakfast sandos.

Once you've had your fill of breakfast, move on to some of their regular menu items. The Pork Banh Mi is the perfect combination of creamy sauce, spiced pork, hot jalapeños, and sweet pickled veggies. If you're looking for a classic, you can't go wrong with a Stock Burger—loaded with all of the

Stockyard has a rotating special every day that is usually there for one day only.

toppings. Pair your burger with their legendary onion rings, which are soft, perfectly light and crispy, and gigantic. If you're feeling carnivorous, grab a braised beef sandwich covered in gooey, melty cheese. Pair that with their home fries, which are crispier and chunkier than your typical side of fries.

The inspiration behind Stockyard's delicious sandwich lineup is the concept of a staff meal, which, if you've ever worked in a restaurant, you know is a meal of "whatever's left" from that day's dishes. Stockyard emphasizes a no-waste style of cooking that utilizes and highlights parts of the animal that others may shy away from. Luckily, Stockyard is run by talented butchers, chefs, and sandwich innovators, so we can all reap the benefits, staff or not.

2

RYBREAD

RYBREAD is a quaint shop that perfectly embodies the neighborhood charm of the Fairmount area. From the homemade baked goods to the delicious sandwiches in a cozy space right on Fairmount Avenue, it's a favorite spot for locals and visitors to grab a snack. All of the sandwiches and salads have quirky names, mostly named after cities that inspired that combination of ingredients. For this stop, I recommend trying a sandwich, since bread is literally in their name. However, we're not talking about any old sandwich, we're talking about the Savannah.

You know the wafting aromas of turkey in the oven, fresh cranberry

sauce being made, and cheesy potatoes on the horizon on Thanksgiving? Well, take all of those happy feelings and throw them between two slices of bread and you have the Savannah, aka the Thanksgiving Sandwich, which you can get year-round at Rybread. This sandwich features oven-roasted turkey breast, brie, whole-cranberry sauce, and mayo on whole-grain bread, and it's the perfect sweet, salty, creamy combo that you love about Thanksgiving. Wash it down with one of their house-made smoothies or coffees, and grab a cupcake for the road!

3

TELA'S MARKET & KITCHEN

The next stop on your Fairmount food journey takes you to TELA'S MARKET & KITCHEN, which is a hybrid specialty market and casual eatery, emphasizing fresh, seasonal ingredients and wholesome options. The first thing you'll notice is that it's literally a market—so if you're looking to stock up on any produce, deli items, or grab-and-go snacks, then you're in luck. However, if you're here to eat, then you're also in luck, because they serve up delicious food as well.

If coffee is your thing, they make tasty drinks—the oat milk mocha is a personal favorite, because it's rich but not overly sweet. Once you have a beverage for the wait, order some dishes to share. If it's still breakfast time, the breakfast burrito is killer—it has the traditional Mexican flavors you

love, perfectly paired with fluffy eggs and a side of crispy potatoes. Next, the Achiote Chicken Tacos are filled with seasoned chicken, salsa roja, caramelized pineapple, onions, cilantro, shredded lettuce, and sour cream on flour tortillas for a sweet and spicy bite. If you're still hungry, grab a pastry from their pastry case (they often have interesting flavors of scones that rotate) as you stroll down Fairmount to your next destination.

4

PIZZERIA VETRI

PIZZERIA VETRI opened in 2013 on 20th and Callowhill and has been a neighborhood mainstay for Philadelphians and visitors alike ever since. Using fresh, seasonal ingredients to create unexpected flavor combinations and carrying an extensive list of beers, wines, and cocktails, Pizzeria Vetri is the neighborhood pizza joint reimagined.

Any proper visit to Pizzeria Vetri has to start with a rotolo—their delicious concoction of pizza dough, ricotta, mortadella, and pistachio pesto rolled into a perfect little bun. This beloved app is creamy, cheesy, hearty, salty, and crunchy all at the same time. If you're looking to be more waistline conscious—try one of the salads, which rotate to reflect what's in season.

Now—perhaps the most important aspect of your visit—the pizza. Pizzeria Vetri's dough has a fermentation process of about four days before it's

used. This dough proves that good things come to those who wait, as it makes for a flawlessly crispy yet chewy crust. If you're wondering what pies to try (though, you really can't go wrong with any of them), this blogger recommends a classic Margherita, a Crudo pie, and a Rock Shrimp pie (so you cover all of your bases with plain, meat, and seafood pies). The Margherita is a classic done right and has the deliciously sweet sauce and hearty chunks of fresh mozzarella that has made it a staple menu item. The Crudo features prosciutto crudo (that gets deliciously crispy in the oven), buffalo mozzarella, and Parmesan cheese, and is salty, cheesy, and indulgent. Lastly, the Rock Shrimp pie features generous chunks of rock shrimp with a tangy salsa verde sauce, making for one of the most unique (and darn tasty) pizza combos out there.

Oh, you thought we were done? You can't leave Pizzeria Vetri without trying one of their signature desserts—Fried Pizza Dough with Nutella. Take chunks of Pizzeria Vetri's already delicious dough, fry them, coat them in citrus fennel sugar, dunk them in Nutella, and you're in for a seriously sweet ending. (*Tip:* The fried dough is a great dish to share!)

5

A MANO

A Mano, which literally translates to "by hand," is all about hand-made cuisine. A quintessential Philadelphia BYOB, A Mano draws from local farms and purveyors to create Italian dishes that are as beautiful as they are delicious.

Start your meal with some homemade focaccia, which is perfectly soft, chewy, and rich. Next, enjoy a salad for a fresh, crisp bite. If the beets are on the menu—get them. Paired with cherries and pistachios, it's a unique preparation that pays off big time. Now, for the main event—pasta. All the pasta. Preparation will change seasonally, but I can confidently say it

will be delicious no matter when you visit. The Mafaldine with Pork Ragu is tender, deliciously salty, and the texture is absolute perfection. The gnocchi are pillowy soft, and the lumache with seasonal mushrooms is a beautiful ode to local produce.

Wrap up your meal with a house-made dessert. The Tiramisu Semifreddo is a unique twist on an Italian classic, marrying tiramisu's flavors with a totally different texture. The lemon olive oil cake is also a deliciously rich treat with a great zing!

6

If you ask any Fairmount local where to get sushi, it's likely that UMAI UMAI is on top of their list. It's a small (like fifteen tables small) sushi restaurant that serves some of the most inventive sushi in the city. Strawberries in a dragon roll? Check. Rolls with nuts? Check. Oyster shooters? You bet. This is a spot to step outside of your sushi comfort zone and try something you normally wouldn't—I can almost guarantee it'll be delicious.

You must start your meal with their crispy brussel sprouts salad, which features various veggies and a sweet chili-tamarind dressing, meaning a sweet, spicy, crunchy bite every time. Next, knock back some oyster shooters (which, even if you don't like oysters, you'll probably like). They're set in a citrus soy sauce with quail egg "bombers"—meaning

a burst of creamy egg yolk with your oyster and uni. It's as umami as it gets. For sushi, designer rolls are where it's at. The Pingu roll is a fan favorite that sort of tastes like a crab rangoon—it's a deep-fried cream cheese and crab roll, with a potato chip crunch topping. If you prefer it raw, the 4-8-15-16-23-42 roll is as fun to eat as it is to say—it's an array of carefully prepared raw fish wrapped in pickled daikon instead of rice, which is a great way to mix things up. Next, grab a Godzilla roll, which is like a Dragon roll with a twist—eel, avocado, and strawberries + nuts (yes, it's weird, and yes, it's good). Lastly, wrap your meal up with a Krakken roll, which may just be the oddest of the bunch—shrimp tempura, eel, avocado, soft-shell crab, cherries, and a Worcestershire sauce aioli. The sweetness of the cherries plus the creamy aioli perfectly complement the fried seafood in this over-the-top roll that perfectly sums up what Umai Umai is about.

If you have any room left for dessert, grab some funnel cake fries before rolling out.

TIP

Umai Umai is BYOB, so bring a nice white to wash down all of the delicious seafood!

THE FISHTOWN CRAWL

1. SURAYA RESTAURANT, 1528 Frankford Ave., Philadelphia, (215) 302-1900, surayaphilly.com

2. FRONT STREET CAFE, 1253 N. Front St., Philadelphia, (215) 515-3073, frontstreetcafe.net

3. LOCO PEZ, 2401 E. Norris St., Philadelphia, (267) 886-8061, locopez.com

4. PIZZERIA BEDDIA, 1313 N. Lee St., Philadelphia, (267) 928-2256

5. MURPH'S BAR, 202 E. Girard Ave., Philadelphia, (215) 425-1847

6. FRANKFORD HALL, 1210 Frankford Ave., Philadelphia, (215) 634-3338, frankfordhall.com

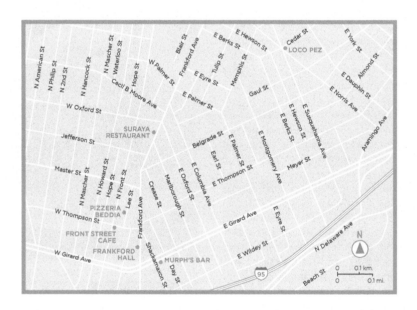

Fishtown

Has nothing to do with fish

If you thought Northern Liberties was hip, then buckle up and get ready to meet NoLib's cool neighbor, the Fishtown neighborhood. Truly an area on the rise, it has emerged as a cultural center of art, music, and, of course, food. Fishtown, which gets its name from its history in the fishing industry, boasts some of the city's best eats, drinks, and sights. Philly's young creatives tend to flock to Fishtown to put down roots, which has led to the boom of new studios, galleries, bars, and restaurants. The narrow streets intertwined with old homes and new architecture alike make it a fascinating region of the city to explore, especially for creatives and foodies.

1

SURAYA RESTAURANT

Yalla! is something you'll likely hear at SURAYA, the all-day market, cafe, restaurant, and garden from the minds behind Cafe la Maude (another delicious stop on the Northern Liberties Food Crawl) and R&D. Nathalie Richan and Roland Kassis (Cafe la Maude) teamed up with Greg Root and Nick Kennedy (R&D) to open one of Philly's most anticipated restaurants in 2018, and one of the most beloved restaurants beyond then. "Yalla" literally translates to "come on," as in "come on and enjoy some delicious Middle Eastern food," which is exactly what you're about to do.

First off, before you even think about what to eat for breakfast, you must get a drink here. While their cocktail bar is delightful, it's likely a little early to slam hard liquor, so indulge in a Lebanese Chai Latte (which comes beautifully adorned with dried edible flowers) or a Tehina Hot Chocolate, which is a delightfully nutty twist on a classic (and comes topped with housemade cotton candy). To ease into your meal, try the Mezze Plate, which comes with labne (strained yogurt with cucumber, olive, mint, tomato, and long hots), a six-minute egg crusted in delicious herbs and spices, cashew dukkah, and Suraya's famous pita. Your jaw can't help but drop when you see their pita come out—perfectly round and almost inflated looking—it's perfectly soft and just thick enough to take on their dips. If you're up for it, grab a plate of baba ghanoush as well, which is excellent here. Topped with pomegranate seeds, it's a great mix of smoky eggplant, nutty tehina,

and sweetness from the fruit. For the main event, the Gravlax Man'oushe is the smoked salmon breakfast pizza you didn't know you needed. The pizza is loaded with house-cured salmon, labne in place of cream cheese, red onion, long hots, and a healthy dose of za'atar spice, taking the classic smoked salmon bagel breakfast to the next level.

Lastly, end your meal on a sweet note with a pastry (or a pastry basket) from the cafe. The Rose & Pistachio Cruller is beloved by many and likely to sell out, so if you see it, grab it. The Linzer Bar is a unique take on a classic Linzer tart, with tehina, almond, and mulberry, while the ma'Amoul cookies, which come with date, walnut, or pistachio filling, are soft, buttery, and extremely tasty. If you're looking for something to pair with some coffee (you'll want to caffeinate for today's food marathon), try the coffee cake, which is made with labne and seven spice, for an ethnic twist on a classic. Now that you've had a taste of the Middle East, get ready to head over to Front Street to keep the brunch bacchanal going.

2 FRONT STREET CAFE

This unassuming cafe sits beneath an underpass, which can make it easy to drive by without realizing that some of the area's tastiest food is available inside. FRONT STREET CAFE cranks out healthy, sustainable, delectable cuisine daily, utilizing local, plant-based, farm-to-table, organic ingredients whenever possible.

Start your meal with the famed buffalo cauliflower. Not to be dramatic, but if they ever took it off the menu, there would likely be an uprising in the city; and if that's not enough to convince you to try it, then I'm not sure what is. Generous chunks of cauliflower are breaded and deep-fried, tossed in your choice of sauce (buffalo is a personal favorite, but they also do garlic-sriracha or General Tso sauce), and they're so good you won't

miss traditional buffalo wings (promise). For a main course, the Gravlax Platter is excellent if you're here around breakfast time. It comes "build-your-own" style, with an everything English muffin, cured salmon, chive cream cheese, and tomatoes, cucumbers, avocado, capers, and pickled onions on the side, so you can make it your way. If you're looking for something a bit heartier, the All-Natural Buttermilk Fried Chicken Sandwich is a home run. All-natural chicken is expertly breaded and fried, topped with a mustard maple aioli, pickles, and butter lettuce, all on a toasted brioche bun. If you're feeling it, you can add applewood bacon or avocado (do both—you only live once). Wash it all down with some coffee or house-made juice, and get ready to keep the party rolling as you take your taste buds south of the border at the next stop.

3

LOCO PEZ

Did you ever think you'd get phenomenal Mexican food in an old-school dive bar? No? Well then, you're in for a treat. First off, yes, LOCO PEZ literally translates to "Crazy Fish." Aptly named, as it resides on the northern border of Fishtown and is full of crazy-loyal patrons who love hanging by the bar, knocking back local brews with delicious tacos. Old-school photos and art line the walls at this dark neighborhood taqueria, which whips out LA-style street food.

To have the full experience, you must order a drink and a plate of

nachos and experience the "oh my gosh" moment when they bring the dish out. A massive tower of crispy tortilla chips is adorned with beans, pico, pickled jalapeños, cheese, sour cream, and scallions. If you happen to come during happy hour, you can typically snag these for half price. As you nosh on your nachos, place an order for a few tacos, and definitely get a variety to try the different options. The

TIP

Loco Pez is cash only but has an ATM on-site.

Crispy Shrimp Taco (*camarones*) is served with shredded cabbage, crema, and pico de gallo. It's crunchy and hearty yet light and fresh all at the same time. For something heavier, the Al Pastor and Pollo Tinga (chicken) are both excellent—melt-in-your mouth meat is topped with cilantro and onions, because sometimes, simple really is best. Now, wipe that crema off your chin, and get ready to dive into some of the best pizza in the city (and the country).

4 PIZZERIA BEDDIA

PIZZERIA BEDDIA has received national acclaim for having not only some of Philly's best pizza, but according to *Time* magazine, it's one of the nineteen best places to eat *in the world*. Yes, you read that correctly—you can literally get some of the best food in the world in Philadelphia. Every publication from *Eater* to *Esquire* to *Bon Appetit* has raved about Pizzeria Beddia at some point, and the hype is well deserved, as every bite at this restaurant, as simple as it may be, is packed with such flavor that you'll fully understand why this place is packed at all hours, day in and day out.

Start your meal with any of the small plates. However, be sure that the Tomato Pie is one of them. At $4 a slice, it's a modest price to pay for one of the most delicious things I've ever tasted. Perfectly

Pizzeria Beddia has a private dining space called The Hoagie Room, where for $75 per person, you can get a private pizza and hoagie *omakase* experience. Talk about cool. The ticketed price of $75 per person includes a welcome cocktail, several small plates, a variety of hoagies from hoagie master John Walker, pizzas, and Beddia's signature soft-serve.

buttery, thick crust holds up a delicately sweet tomato sauce, and a hefty spritz of olive oil takes you on a journey straight to Italy. Once you've licked your fingers, it's time for the main event: pizza. You have to try a classic—so get the plain pie with tomato and whole-milk mozzarella (and add some pepperoni if that's your thing). From the crispy crust to the melty cheese to the simple tomato sauce—it's really the perfect pizza. While the classics at Beddia are delicious, it's really the specials that shine. Joe

Beddia, the mastermind behind the pizzeria, cranks out crazy pizza concoctions on a rotating basis, and they're sure to wow. Pictured here was a special with kale and a cherry reduction, which when paired with the creamy white base made for a magically tangy, smoky, indulgent bite that I'm frankly still thinking about. Any proper meal at Pizzeria Beddia has to end with some house-made soft-serve before you head on to your next stop for some mind-blowing pasta!

5

MURPH'S BAR

You might be surprised to learn that some of Philly's best Italian food comes from an Irish Pub in Fishtown. Yes, you read that correctly. MURPH'S is an Irish pub, complete with exposed brick, quirky decor, and a total neighborhood feel. The setup is interesting—you have Murph's actual bar, which is a standard bar with plenty of drink options. However, adjacent to the bar is an eighteen-seat dining room where you can get some of the most delicious Italian food in the city. The chef behind Murph's, Francesco Bellastelli, is indeed Italian, and he rents the kitchen from the bar and handles the food and food sales (which are cash only). He's there six nights a week cranking out Italian favorites.

Any proper meal at Murph's should start with the deep-fried burrata, which is a level of decadence you didn't know you could achieve. The crispy outer shell makes way for creamy, warm burrata and perfectly flavorful fresh mozzarella cheese, topped in a

TIP

Reservations are only taken for parties of six or more, so you should expect a wait.

delightfully sweet tomato sauce that's sure to linger in your mind for days to come. Next, the meatballs are exquisite. Perfectly tender, perfectly seasoned, and just like Nonna used to make, only better. Now, make way for

some pasta, because that's what Murph's does best.

As if gnocchi weren't delicious enough on its own—Chef Bellastelli went ahead and created stuffed gnocchi, which is topped with tomato sauce and a literal pile of ricotta salata. The texture is soft and pillowy, with tons of cheesy flavor. Next, the truffle pasta is a must. It's creamy, dreamy, and loaded with truffle so every bite transports you right to Italy. Lastly, the Pear and Cheese Fiocchi is something that you'll dream about for weeks after having it. Little purses of pasta reveal a delicate mixture of cheese and pear, and the dish is served in a Parmesan cream with a drizzle of honey, for a pasta so good, it's basically dinner and dessert in one.

6 FRANKFORD HALL

Raise your stein glass in the air and get ready for tasty eats and killer beers at FRANKFORD HALL, an old-style biergarten for the twenty-first century. Set in the heart of the Fishtown neighborhood, Frankford Hall is an industrial-chic building with a huge outdoor beer garden that welcomes guests to have a seat, have a (oftentimes large) beer, and stay a while.

First things first, get yourself a beer. Frankford Hall cleverly divides up their menu by beer tastes: Funky & Tart for sours and gose beers, Dark & Savory for stouts and porters, etc. With beer in hand, guests typically pick up a game of Jenga and enjoy a few laughs with their friends, eventually scarfing down one of Frankford Hall's infamous soft pretzels. The Riesenpretzel (giant pretzel) is a late-night staple (and on the late-night menu), because nothing goes better with a beer. Frankford cranks these out until 1:30 a.m., so it's the perfect place to end your night. If you're in need of some more serious eats, the kitchen also cranks out an entire menu of sausages (bratwurst, frankfurters, you name it) until late. So, grab your friends, grab a beer, and give a big "Prost!" to ending your Fishtown food tour.

TIP

Outdoor seating is all picnic tables, so it's perfect for bringing a group.

THE MANAYUNK CRAWL

1. WINNIE'S MANAYUNK, **4266 Main St., Philadelphia, (215) 487-2663,** winniesmanayunk.com

2. THE GOAT'S BEARD, **4201 Main St., Philadelphia, (267) 323-2495,** thegoatsbeardphilly.com

3. TUBBY ROBOT ICE CREAM FACTORY, **4369 Main St., Philadelphia, (267) 423-4376, tubbyrobot.com**

4. JAKE'S & COOPER'S WINE BAR, **4365 Main St., Philadelphia, (215) 483-0444, jakesandcoopers.com**

5. LUCKY'S LAST CHANCE, **4421 Main St., Philadelphia, (215) 509-6005,** luckyslastchance.com

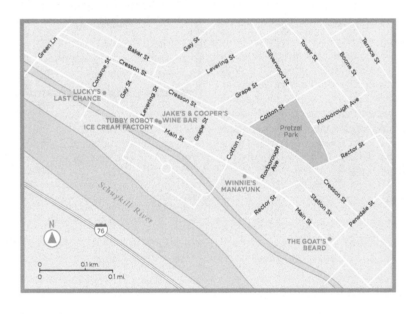

Manayunk

Urban setting with small-town charm

Manayunk boasts Victorian homes, lofts, old row homes, and many lifelong residents who love the feeling of home just outside the bustle of the city. Manayunk is now known for Main Street, which is lined with restaurants offering delicious fare, fun bars, and unique cafes and stores that delight residents and visitors alike. With the Schuylkill River on one side and bustling storefronts on the other, it's the perfect blend of urban and suburban, where everyone feels at home.

1 WINNIE'S MANAYUNK

If you ask someone where to get breakfast in Manayunk, you're likely to hear about Winnie's, a Main Street institution. Winnie Clowry grew up watching her father cook, and she took a restaurant job in Manayunk in 1994. In 2003 Winnie and her husband purchased the restaurant, situated in a historic mill, and Winnie's was born. Known for generous portions, friendly service, and their homemade jam— WINNIE'S is where any proper Manayunk crawl should start.

Like any proper breakfast, alcohol should be involved. Winnie's Bloody Mary comes appropriately

spicy with a big piece of crispy bacon in it, so enjoy that while you wait on your food. You'll get a pastry basket and jam for the table while you wait, and frankly, this may be your favorite part of the meal, because the homemade jam at Winnie's is *that* good. Try it on the various breads (the corn bread being my personal favorite) and then think to yourself, "Wow, no other jam matters anymore."

For mains you can go the sweet or savory route. If you're feeling savory, try eggs Benedict or build your own omelet. If you're feeling sweet, you'll likely enjoy the classic waffles with fruit or the crème brûlée French toast, which comes loaded with cream filling, berries, and whipped cream. Who says you can't have dessert for breakfast?

2

THE GOAT'S BEARD

Sean Coyle grew up in the restaurant business, with his parents owning more than thirty restaurants in Philly from the 1960s to the 2000s, so opening THE GOAT'S BEARD in Manayunk came naturally to him in 2013. Since then, it's quickly become a favorite for locals and out-of-towners alike for its inventive menus and killer cocktails. A restaurant that prides itself in sourcing premium and sourcing local, The Goat's Beard puts a high-end spin on comfort classics.

First and foremost, you are doing yourself a major disservice if you do not try their mac and cheese, which is made with potato gnocchi and a homemade cheese sauce that you'll want to bathe in. As if the gnocchi aren't delicious enough on their own, the creamy, flavorful cheese sauce

and crunchy bread-crumb topping takes this dish to the next level. Know what goes well with mac and cheese? Chicken nuggets. That's right, we're on a second-grade diet—but this is the adult version of it, because The Goat's Beard nuggets are putting a serious twist on a childhood favorite. They take premium chicken and bread it in a house-made, spiced blend, and the fried chicken is coated in a sweet sriracha sauce, topped with blue cheese and scallions, and voilà— nuggets *elevated*. They're sweet, spicy, cheesy, tangy, crunchy, and all-around wonderful. Lastly, any proper lunch has a sandwich component, and The Goat's Beard's turkey club is *the* sandwich. This

TIP

If you come back for dinner, you can get their gnocchi mac & cheese as an entree with sliced steak on top—booyah!

turkey club has house-smoked pork belly (in generous slabs), roast turkey, avocado spread, house-made aioli, and frisée for some crunch—it combines textures and flavors in a way that will make every other turkey club you've had seem like a middle-school cafeteria lunch.

3

THE TUBBY ROBOT ICE CREAM FACTORY

Brainchild of native Philadelphians Chris Maguire and Steve Wright Jr., THE TUBBY ROBOT, aside from being an adorable mascot, is an ice cream parlor unlike any other. Not only do they specialize in delicious homemade ice cream (all sourced from local dairy) and unique sundae combinations, but they focus on cultivating a love for gaming, so yes, you can literally eat ice cream and play video games just like your ten-year-old self always dreamt of. Owners Chris and Steve state that "Nothing brings us more joy than watching the newest generation of kids play arcade games and loving them. We get to expose young folks to an arcade culture that is in very short supply in the modern world, and it's fascinating to see how cross-generational it really is."

Start with a waffle sundae—for two reasons. One, it lets you try four different ice cream flavors at once. Two, it's served on a fresh-made Belgian waffle, so it's basically a balanced meal. As much as I want to pick a favorite flavor, it's next to impossible because they're all crazy good—the perfect creamy, soft consistency, bursting with real flavor. Post waffle, it's time for dessert (yes, post-dessert dessert is a thing when you're on a food crawl). The brownie sundae is a must. Chewy, fudgy brownie base, delicious ice cream (I recommend their dark chocolate flavor), and whipped topping make for a truly decadent treat. Hang out by the Wall-o-Vision, a custom-built gaming installation, and play some curated classic arcade games while you enjoy your treat.

4 JAKE'S & COOPER'S WINE BAR

When Jake's Restaurant opened in 1987, contemporary American cuisine was still a new concept to the area. There were far fewer dining options than there are today, so the restaurant opened with a focus on sauce work, treating protein with the utmost respect, and making everything in-house. All of that still holds true today.

Bruce Cooper opened Jake's Restaurant with an impressive, refined menu and a thoughtfully curated wine list, which caught the attention of numerous food critics and earned the restaurant a number of prestigious awards. For more than three decades, Jake's has been serving the patrons of Philadelphia fresh, delicious fare (with

fantastic wine). With an extensive menu of light bites and an awesome daily happy hour, JAKE'S AND COOPER'S WINE BAR is the perfect pre-dinner stop when touring Manayunk.

Start with a glass of white (or red—they have thirty wines by the glass) and the tuna tartare, which pairs fresh fish with avocado and grapefruit for a delicate, citrusy bite. Next, try the crab cake, which has been a menu staple for decades and continues to wow patrons new and old. The gnocchi are also a hit—with bright, herbal flavors and a hearty sauce, it's the perfect balance of filling but not too filling. Lastly, get their mussels (red). The sauce is light enough to not overpower the mussels (which are as fresh as can be) but still adds a great flavor, and you'll enjoy slurping them down with one more glass of vino before you head on to your next stop.

5 LUCKY'S LAST CHANCE

LUCKY'S LAST CHANCE opened in 2011, mixing a cool dive-bar atmosphere with a passion for burgers and beer. Upon opening, the team had a goal to sell twenty burgers a night. As word spread, they quickly exceeded their goals and set new ones—to be the destination for burger lovers in Philadelphia. Now locals and out-of-towners alike enjoy their array of burgers, hot dogs, mac and cheese, and more.

Naturally, this is a place where you need to order a burger (or three). The Incomparable Bacon Cheddar burger (yes, that's really its name) is really incomparable—two patties, onion, cheddar cheese, bacon, BBQ sauce, *and* sriracha aioli—yeah, it's loaded. Once you've enjoyed that, wipe the BBQ sauce off your face and get ready for a fiesta in your mouth, because the El Guapo burger tastes like all of your favorite Mexican flavors rolled into one. This burger has pepper jack cheese, guacamole, sour cream, diced tomato, jalapeños, and crispy tortilla chips for a deliciously creamy, cheesy, spicy, crunchy bite.

Now it's time for the grand finale—the PB & Bacon burger, which is the three-time People's Choice Winner at the Philadelphia Burger Brawl (an annual event that brings together some of the best burgers in Philadelphia to determine whose is best). This burger is unlike any you've ever had—because it combines a delicious double bacon cheeseburger with a childhood classic: PB&J. You read that right—this burger literally has two patties, bacon, cheese, and then peanut butter and grape jelly, which makes for an unexpectedly decadent bite. It's creamy, sweet, salty, smoky, cheesy, meaty—all at once. It may sound odd (I mean, it is), but it's a perfect example of the unapologetically gluttonous nature of Lucky's Last Chance.

THE NORTHERN LIBERTIES CRAWL

1. DOLCE & CAFFE, **708 N. 2nd St., Philadelphia, (215) 627-1130,** dolceandcaffe.com

2. THE KETTLE BLACK, **631 N. 2nd St., Philadelphia,** thekettleblackphilly.com

3. CAFE LA MAUDE, **816 N. 4th St., Philadelphia, (267) 318-7869,** cafelamaude.com

4. ONE SHOT CAFE, **217 W. George St., Philadelphia, (215) 627-1620**

5. LOVE & HONEY FRIED CHICKEN, **1100 N. Front St., Philadelphia, (215) 789-7878, loveandhoneyfriedchicken.com**

6. APRICOT STONE, **1040 N. American St., Philadelphia, (267) 606-6596,** apricotstonephilly.com

7. YARDS BREWING COMPANY, **500 Spring Garden St., Philadelphia, (215) 525-0175, yardsbrewing.com**

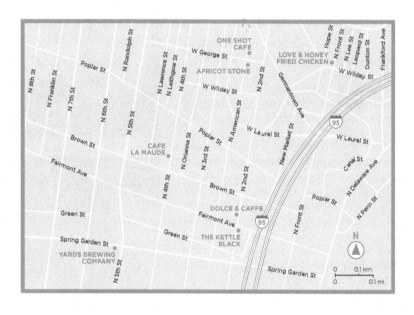

Northern Liberties

Hip people, hipper food

Northern Liberties (affectionately called NoLibs here in Philly) has long been referred to as an "up and coming" area. Well, the time has come, and NoLibs has up and come. This neighborhood connects Old City and Fishtown, and it really is the perfect blend of both. Hip yet refined, NoLibs has everything from quirky bars to tech firms on the rise, with a young, fun population to match. Locals flock to the area for its cheap studio space, fun bars, and delicious eats. While yes, you'll often see rolled jeans with funky socks, flat-brim hats, tiny glasses, and foot-long beards, NoLibs isn't nearly as "hipster" as it gets made out to be. Rather, it's a neighborhood that perfectly blends cool cuisine and hip hangouts with an air of approachability that makes it a great place for any-one to visit.

1 When coming to Northern Liberties, you must start your day at Dolce & Caffe. This adorable coffee shop is tucked toward the end of a row of bars, restaurants, and shops, and people are constantly popping in and out for a quick bite and a fantastic cup of coffee. Dolce & Caffe is the product of Italian immigrants who were looking to create a cafe that was true to their Italian roots and culture, and they've hit the mark with Dolce & Caffe.

Start your day with one of their specialty coffees like a creamy, indulgent Nutella latte. Pair that latte with one of their delicious grab-and-go breakfast items or pastries and you're sure to start your day on a high note. Their bomboloni are light, fluffy, and bursting with ricotta and Nutella flavor. They also make some of the best cannoli in the city. They make just about everything fresh in-house, and the few

Dolce's BEST:
Sicilian Cannoli
mini $2.50 mini dipped $3.00
regular $5.00 regular $6.00
or GET A CATERING dipped
TRAY!!

things that they don't are imported directly from Italy. In the case of the cannoli, the shells come from Italy and the ricotta filling is made in-house. They're the perfect blend of crunchy, creamy, and just sweet enough. If you're looking for more substance, try their Strawberry Ricotta Waffle. Fresh-made waffles are topped with that delicious house-made ricotta filling, strawberries, and syrup for a truly decadent breakfast. If savory breakfasts are more your speed, try a breakfast sandwich. Even their simple bacon, egg, cheese, and avocado on kaiser roll is sure to please even the pickiest eaters.

TIP

You can get anything wrapped up to go if you can't get a seat in this tiny cafe, but if you're looking to grab a seat, come before 11 a.m. on weekends.

2 If you ask any NoLibs local where to grab a quick bite, odds are THE KETTLE BLACK is going to be mentioned in their top three. This micro-bakery focuses on quality over quantity, cranking out French-inspired breads, pastries, and bagels that taste as good as they look. The brainchild of husband-and-wife duo Marc (who is French born and raised) and Claire (who lived in France), the two put their passion for good bread and delicious coffee together and opened The Kettle Black as a way to share that with their community.

The first thing you'll notice upon walking in is the bread and pastry cases, both of which are brimming

with some seriously beautiful baked goods. From unique flavor combos in their breads to the sweet stuff, everything is baked in-house daily. While you scan the pastry case with your mouth open (or is that just me?), grab a delicious house-crafted espresso from one of their expertly trained baristas. Nothing pairs better with carbs than delicious coffee, and boy is the coffee at The Kettle Black delicious. First, you must try one of their breads—whether it's a baguette, a loaf, or focaccia. The care and precision that goes into baking any and every thing at The Kettle Black is evident in every bite (promise). Next, order a signature black bagel, which is an absolute must (bonus: they're super-Instagrammable). Whether you're feeling plain cream cheese or a lox sandwich, the black bagel is the perfect complement. Next, you must try the croissant, which is easily one of the best in Philadelphia. The croissant is flaky, buttery, and beyond delicious. Lastly, end your visit on a sweet note with a donut brioche, which is essentially a cross between a brioche bun and a donut doused in homemade glaze and sprinkles.

Every baked good at The Kettle Black uses sourdough as a leavening agent, which, for non-bakers, means that every product takes at least twenty-four hours from start to finish. However, once you try the breads and baked goods here, you'll realize that some things are worth waiting for.

3

CAFE LA MAUDE

What do you get when you mix French and Lebanese cuisines? You get one of Philly's best brunch spots, duh. Lucky for you (and the rest of the world), CAFE LA MAUDE serves brunch all day, with an eclectic menu that truly showcases both French and Lebanese cuisines through healthy, hearty food. Owners Nathalie and Gabi started Cafe la Maude as a coffee shop in Northern Liberties intending to serve coffee and snacks inspired by Nathalie's upbringing. Her mother owned a restaurant in Liberia for forty-five years. Meanwhile, Gabi grew up in Syria, where he developed his passion for food and community. Fast-forward to now, and Cafe la Maude has gone from offering two or three small items to an entire menu—they've become a community staple.

What's particularly great about the menu at Cafe la Maude is that it features dishes that are heavily Middle East influenced, dishes that are super-French, and dishes that are a blend of both. When stopping by, take your taste buds on a trip around the world and try a bit of everything. Start with a chai latte, which is made in-house and pairs perfectly with a little treat from their pastry case. For savory brunch items, you cannot leave without trying the Parisian Za, one of their most popular dishes (for good reason). An open-faced pizza croissant is topped with caramelized onions, avocado, and French ham that has warm goat cheese rolled into the center. Served with a side of fries, salad, and fruit, this dish hits all of the flavor notes you want (and those that you didn't know you wanted). Next, try the Green Shakshuka, which is Nathalie's take on a traditional shakshuka dish (eggs baked in a tomato sauce). Hers is made with onions, peppers, green tomatoes, spinach, and kale, topped with fried veggies and a carrot tahini sauce and warm breaded feta. El Beit is another great traditional dish. It is egg based and topped with assorted roasted vegetables, salad, and whipped feta. End your visit on a sweet note with the Pomme Caramel—lemon ricotta pancakes with apples and homemade caramel, topped with shaved chocolate and pistachios.

4 ONE SHOT CAFE

Opened in 2005, ONE SHOT CAFE can be described as a true neighborhood fixture. Built into the corner of a cozy row of homes is this funky, edgy, downright delicious coffee shop named in homage to the owner's grandfather, who served in the Air Force.

From the upstairs library to the communal table built around a real motorcycle, One Shot is oozing with cool. Owner Melissa is a one-woman show who does everything from blending beans to crafting menus to handling the day-to-day operations of the cafe. She has created a completely unique, completely welcoming space in the heart of Northern

Liberties where vegans and carnivores alike can come together over good food and great coffee. All menu items are farm-to-table and sourced locally, with an emphasis on fresh flavors that let the ingredients shine. If you come here early, try the French toast (and share it with your friends)—soft, chewy toast meets dulce de leche sauce, spiced nuts, and a salted honey butter for a sweet start to your day. If it's a bit later in the day, try one of the rotating varieties of avocado toast (pictured is the toast with feta, asparagus, and roasted chickpeas) or a seasonal grain bowl. The grain bowl packs a flavorful punch with spiced grains, salad, fresh blackberries and blueberries, and half an avocado. All together, the dish is fresh, light, and satisfying (and you can always add an egg or meat to the dish to make it heartier).

When visiting One Shot, don't skip the java. Melissa has a rich background as a barista and a serious passion for a good cup of coffee, so One Shot has a vast and unique menu of caffeinated (and non-caffeinated) beverages. Their Oat Milk and Honey Latte with cinnamon is a best seller (and for good reason)—it's creamy, sweet, and bursting with flavor. One Shot also makes one of the best chai

TIP

Sit downstairs for prime people-watching, or head upstairs for a more intimate, private setting.

lattes in the city, using a proprietary chai blend that they steep for hours into a concentrate and then mix with steamed milk to create what literally tastes like a hug in a mug.

5 LOVE & HONEY FRIED CHICKEN

Love & Honey's story is more of a love story than anything—the love story of Todd and Laura Lyons. The two met at the Culinary Institute of America, hit it off, and ended up married. After establishing themselves in the food industry, in 2015 the two decided that they were ready to start their own venture, so LOVE & HONEY FRIED CHICKEN was born. Now the two proudly serve fried chicken that is brined for eight hours, dredged in buttermilk and seasoned flour, deep fried, and always served with a drizzle of honey before serving (aka made with love).

The first thing you try, naturally, has to be the fried chicken. Try a few different pieces—thigh, drumstick, etc. Each piece is crispy, tender, and just slightly sweet, and they pair great with a buttery corn muffin. Next, the Nashville Hot Chicken Sandwich is a showstopper. The sandwich starts with spicy buttermilk fried chicken, which is topped with ranch slaw, sweet pickles, and ranch on a toasted brioche bun. The sweet brioche, tangy pickles, creamy ranch, and cool slaw perfectly balance the heat of the chicken, which is loaded with flavor. It's a sandwich you're sure to think about time and time again. Now, you might think this place only makes chicken—but they actually have excellent house-made desserts. They have cookies and pies that rotate seasonally, and you should absolutely try whatever is in season. Pictured is a classic sweet

potato pie with marshmallow topping, which is creamy, lightly sweet, and decadent. Cookies are baked fresh every day, and they're available until they sell out! Now get ready for a radical change of cuisine as we step into the world of Middle Eastern eats.

6 APRICOT STONE

Part of me was hesitant to include APRICOT STONE in this crawl solely because I think this place is one of Philly's best-kept secrets. The menu is simple, straightforward, and reasonably priced, and the food is phenomenal. To boot, it's BYOB, which means that you can save your dollars for another order of dolma (which you'll likely want). Apricot Stone is a family affair, tucked away behind the famous Piazza and run by a mother (Chef Fimy) and son (Ara) duo from Aleppo, Syria.

Start your meal with (literally all of) their dips. Personal favorites are the hummus, which is thick and creamy; the muhammara, which is made with a house-made pomegranate molasses; and the baba ghanoush, which is fresh and light. Now, for a second round of appetizers (yes, I'm serious), get their falafel, which are arguably some of the best in the city. They're gigantic and could easily be an entree for a vegetarian/vegan friend, but they're also great for sharing. Crunchy on the outside, flavorful and tender on the inside, Apricot Stone has really perfected these. Get an order of dolma too, which are grape leaves stuffed with rice, cheese, and, in this case, a hint of pomegranate molasses, which adds a sweetness that traditional dolma lack. Now, onto some boreg and spanakopita, both of which are flaky, cheesy, and an ideal comfort food. Once you're done licking up the crumbs of your appetizers, it's time for some meats. All of their kebabs are cooked fresh to order, and they're all bursting with flavor from the marinades and spice rubs that the kitchen uses. I highly recommend the luleh kebab, which could best be described as a house-made spiced lamb sausage. If you're a red-meat eater, their filet mignon kebab is notoriously delicious as well.

Now, loosen up your belt by a notch so that you can try some of Apricot Stone's phenomenal, traditional house-made desserts. You can't go wrong with their baklava, which is flaky, sweet, chewy, and nutty all at the same time. My personal favorite is their baklava with cheese, which is much more exciting than it sounds. The inside is essentially a house-made cheesecake filling, topped with crispy phyllo dough and house-made infused syrup, which makes for a bite that's crunchy, creamy, cheesy, and sweet, without being super-heavy. Now get ready to wash down a good day's eats with some killer brews from a Philly legend.

7 YARDS BREWING COMPANY

YARDS BREWING COMPANY is really synonymous with Philly and has been brewing some of the city's most loved beers since way back when, when two college buds, Tom and Jon, decided to brew some beer for their friends. Call it talent or call it dumb luck, but their beer was an instant hit, thus Yards was born in 1994. What started as a garage-sized operation in Manayunk has exploded into a giant brewhouse and taproom in the Northern Liberties section of Philadelphia.

The taproom is a great mix of industrial and rustic, where old meets new. Giant windows open up to abundant outdoor seating on the patio, and inside, patrons circle the giant bar to catch whatever game

is on that day. Throughout the tap-room, groups of friends kick back over a cold one paired with some delicious bar food. Yards distrib-utes throughout the mid-Atlantic region, with nine year-round offer-ings and several seasonal/limited releases that you'll only find at the taproom. One of the best-known brews is the Philadelphia Pale Ale, which is a well-balanced dry-hopped ale that pairs especially well with a soft, chewy, salty pret-zel. The pretzel comes with a side of mustard and beer cheese so that you can alternate your flavors. If you're seeking a sturdy sipper, try the IPA, which is hoppy, smooth, and malty. Lastly, the Loyal Lager is a great in-between choice and pairs great with a big ol' plate of nachos. Now kick back, enjoy some beers, and remember the Yards' motto—"Brew Unto Others," meaning to really take in and enjoy the company you're with. Cheers!

THE OLD CITY CRAWL

1. AMADA, **217-219 Chestnut St., Philadelphia, (215) 398-6968, philadelphia.amadarestaurant.com**

2. CUBA LIBRE RESTAURANT & RUM BAR, **10 S. 2nd St., Philadelphia, (215) 627-0666, cubalibrerestaurant.com**

3. GLORY BEER BAR & KITCHEN, **126 Chestnut St., Philadelphia, (267) 687-7878, gloryphilly.com**

4. THE FRANKLIN FOUNTAIN, **116 Market St., Philadelphia, (215) 627-1899, franklinfountain.com**

5. ROYAL BOUCHERIE, **52 S. 2nd St., Philadelphia, (267) 606-6313, royalboucherie.com**

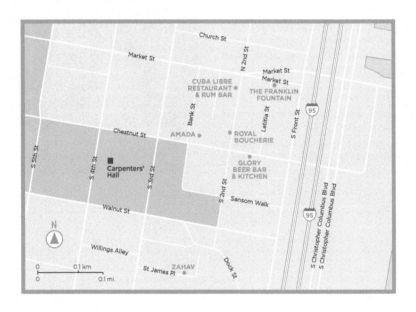

Old City

Historical and delicious

Known for its famous sites from the Colonial era, Old City is really the birthplace of American independence. Home to the Betsy Ross House, Independence Hall, and the Liberty Bell, Old City is a must-visit for any first-time visitor to the city. A paradise for history buffs, Old City boasts more than just sites to see—it's also a food lover's dream. From fun bars to Cuban food to one of the city's best burgers—Old City has a little bit of everything, making it the perfect neighborhood to spend a day in. Stroll through some of the country's oldest streets, marvel at the historical sites and renovated eighteenth-century brownstone homes, and grab a few delicious bites and brews along the way.

1

AMADA

While studying abroad in Madrid as part of his culinary studies at Kendall College, Iron Chef Jose Garces fell in love with Spanish tapas and wrote the business plan for Amada (which translates to "beloved," in honor of his grandmother). AMADA opened its doors in 2005 and has been a culinary icon in the city ever since. Drawing from his Ecuadorian heritage, Chef Garces nurtures a culture of Latin-inspired hospitality paired with bold, authentic flavors, which makes Amada a must-visit in Old City.

Given that it's a tapas restaurant, it's a perfect spot for a group to grab a bunch of plates, try a bit of everything, and really experience an authentic Spanish meal on the East Coast.

Start with the Patatas Bravas, which are bite-sized crispy potatoes served with a creamy paprika aioli. Imagine the best french fries you've ever had and then make them ten times better, and that's what you can expect from the Patatas at Amada. Then, for something a bit heartier (but still light), get an order of Gambas al Ajillo (garlic shrimp), which come with little toasts for creating a crunchy, salty, garlicky bite. The Croquetas de Jamon (ham croquettes served with romesco) are quite likely to be the best you ever eat—creamy, salty, and a bit sweet, they're deep fried to perfection. Lastly, try the ever-popular Chuletas de Cordero (lamb chops), which are prepared with minimal accompaniments to truly let the lamb shine (and boy, does it ever). Spanish cuisine is notorious for simple, fresh flavors, and this lamb knocks it out of the park. Add a squeeze of fresh lemon and enjoy!

One of the best things about Amada? There's a retail area where you can buy everything from Spanish olive oil to Garces's own Garlic Caramel (you read that right) to take home and enjoy. Now, it's time to say *adios* as we move along to the next establishment.

2. CUBA LIBRE RESTAURANT & RUM BAR

As you walk into CUBA LIBRE RESTAURANT & RUM BAR, you can't help but feel like you've stepped back in time into the Cuba of a bygone era. The tropical decor instantly transports you to a street in the center of Old Havana, and the restaurant as a whole celebrates Cuban cuisine and heritage. Since Cuban cuisine is a cultural cauldron composed of many ethnicities, simmered together to create the Criolli (home-style) cuisine of the island, two-time James Beard Award–winning chef-partner Guillermo Pernot's menus feature tastes that reflect Cuba's culinary traditions, as well as the emerging modern cuisine that he has experienced in his ongoing travels to Cuba.

Once you've taken in the gorgeous atmosphere of the restaurant, your eye can't help but wander over to the extensive bar. Cuba Libre holds a Benchmark Award from *Cheers* as the nation's "Best Cocktail Program," and it's clear why. With more than ninety rums in their collection, it's an excellent place to branch out from your usual vodka tonic and try

TIP

In addition to their culinary experience, Cuba Libre transforms into a nightlife venue after dinner on weekends and highlights Latin music and salsa dancing, so bring your dancing shoes!

something fun, like their signature rum drink, the mojito. The mojito is made with sugarcane juice (known as guarapo), which they fresh-press in-house, and lime juice, for a sweet and tangy drink. They make mojitos (as well as their other cocktails) in a variety of fresh fruit flavors, so you can feel like you're in Cuba anytime.

Naturally, you have to pair some snacks with their drinks, and what goes better with a mojito than some guacamole? Their house-made pineapple guacamole is a fruity, sweet take on a classic, and it's served with plantain chips, which play perfectly with the sweetness of the pineapple. For a sweet snack, pastelitos are a must. They're bite-sized puff pastry turnovers filled with cream cheese and guava jam, and they're dusted with powdered sugar for a hint of extra sweetness. Now brush that powdered sugar off your chin, and get ready to keep the party going with another Old City favorite that boasts an impressive collection of brews.

3

GLORY BEER BAR & KITCHEN

Many Philadelphians remember Eulogy Belgian Tavern, which was known for an extensive beer selection in a cool, rustic tavern setting. When it shuttered in 2017, Dave Crudele, the spot's lead bartender and a beer aficionado, was left trying to figure out what to do. By teaming up with his childhood best friend, a financial advisor, and with the support of connected Philadelphians and suburbanites, Dave opened GLORY BEER BAR & KITCHEN. Now, Glory has become a staple in Old City, where everyone from a local tattoo artist to a high-powered exec can come without pretense, enjoy great food and a few awesome beers, listen to some great records on vinyl, and take in all that Old City has to offer.

Start your meal with a cheese-and-charcuterie board, which is constantly changing, so you likely won't get the same combo twice. Then move on to something a bit heavier, like one of the delicious salads. Pictured is an octopus salad with pickled vegetables, but note that the salads often rotate based on what's seasonal. Now for the crown jewel, the porchetta. This sandwich features crispy porchetta that's broiled expertly so it almost tastes like pork crusted in pork rinds. It's served with braised greens and provolone, making it a fantastic Americana twist on a Philly classic flavor combo. Lastly, any proper meal at Glory must involve beer, and there's truly something for everyone. Talk to a bartender to try a few things and find your new favorite. With thirty-six beers on tap (plus another fifty-plus in bottles), they will most definitely find you something you will really like. Enjoy a few brews and the laid-back vibe of Glory before making your way down to our next stop for dinner.

If beer isn't your thing, they also make killer cocktails and have tap lines dedicated to beloved ice cream spots for your next stop.

ICE
CREAMS
Our Own Make

VANILLA
CHOCOLATE
HYDROX COOKIE
MINT CHOC CHIP
PEANUT BUTTER
CHOCOLATE CHIP
COFFEE
ROCKY ROAD
WHIRLY BERLEY
MAPLE WALNUT
PISTACHIO
BUTTER PECAN
CHERRY BUTTER ALMOND
CARAMELIZED BANANA
STRAWBERRY
BLACK RASPBERRY
COCONUT
PEACH
RUM RAISIN
COTTON CANDY
GREEN TEA
TEABERRY

SUG. FREE BUTTER PECAN

DRINKS

ICE CREAM
SODAS
Root Beer Float
Coca Cola & Ice Cream
Wiener Eiskaffee
Ladies' Choice
Cherry Bomb $ 9.

MILKSHAKES
(Any Flavor ~ Malts + $1.)

Regular $ 9.
Large $ 10.

NEW YORK
EGG CREAMS

IC
SP

The Franklin M
Homemade Hot
The Lightning
Mt. Vesuvius

+ + G.

B

Dr. D

Small $ 5⁸⁰

4

THE FRANKLIN FOUNTAIN

In 2004 the Berley brothers opened up THE FRANKLIN FOUNTAIN, an old-timey ice cream parlor where people flock to try their crazy flavors in their retro space. All of the ice cream is handmade and hand-scooped, and the flavor combinations are truly endless. The Fountain offers standard flavors like vanilla bean and Hydrox cookie (cookies and cream) if you're a purist. If you want to get slightly more adventurous, they have flavors like black raspberry (a personal favorite) or honeycomb (seasonal around the summer). If you're feeling wild, try something special like banana (which is actually creamy and delicious), teaberry gum (which tastes like wintermint and has a bright-pink color), or cotton candy (which is a bright-pink ice cream with a blue marshmallow swirl). No matter what you get—slap it on a cone, douse it in sprinkles, and enjoy feeling like a kid again (an old-timey kid, at that). Now, you might think this ends your tour of Old City, but there's one more stop on this historical neighborhood bacchanal.

Honorable Mention: Zahav Restaurant

237 St. James Place, Philadelphia
(215) 625-8800, zahavrestaurant.com

I would be remiss to let you come to this part of Philadelphia and not tell you that you're in close proximity to one of the best restaurants in the nation (actually, the best restaurant in the country according to a 2019 James Beard Award), Zahav. Michael Solomonov and Steve Cook's Israeli restaurant is consistently heralded for its phenomenal, authentic food, killer service, and insanely delicious dessert (from Camille Cogswell, who is also the pastry genius behind K'far Cafe in the Cafe Crawl). Given its extreme popularity, the odds of snagging a walk-in table (especially for a group) are slim to none, but you may be able to snag an elusive seat in this culinary kingdom. If you do come here, opt for the tasting menu and let your taste buds get whisked away to Israel. You'll quickly understand why the James Beard Awards team (and all of Philadelphia) love this spot so dearly.

5

ROYAL BOUCHERIE

Now that you've had a full day of eating, it's time for a proper nightcap, and there's no better spot for a late-night cocktail and delicious snack than French-inspired brasserie Royal Boucherie. Upon entering, you can't help but feel cool at the Boucherie—it's dark, lit mostly by old-timey lights and candles, and is decorated true to its French inspiration. The locally sourced menu boasts everything from house-made pork rinds to one of the best burgers in the city, and the rotating cocktail list is equal parts experimental and approachable.

Start with the French 52, which is a riff on a French 75. Sparkling rosé, rose water, lemon, sugar, and gin make this a tasty, refreshing drink that you could easily crush a few of. If you're feeling more ambitious, try the Philadelphia Fish House Punch, which is a spirit-forward homage to the cocktails of old-time Philadelphia. Jamaican rums, cognac, simple syrup, peach brandy, lemon juice, and lime juice create a delicious flavor blend that truly lets the spirits shine. Royal Boucherie also rotates their cocktail

menu (seasonally, as with the regular menu), so depending on when you stop in, trying something seasonal!

Now, what to pair with your booze? To be honest, you can't go wrong with literally anything here. There's a reason Elmi won *Top Chef*—his food is crazy good. Two personal favorites are the pork chips and the tuna tartare. The pork chips are house-made pork rinds, which are brined so that they get extra puffy and crispy, which, I promise, matters. They're served with a house-made herbed crème fraîche for dipping, which is the perfect accompaniment to the crunchy, meaty rinds. If you're up for it after a full day of eating, get the Boucherie Burger, which is heralded as one of the city's best—with bacon, American cheese, and truffle mayo, it's a decadent, satisfying bite. Given that Royal Boucherie is known for their expert treatment of meats and seafood, it's only right that you try some seafood as well. The tuna tartare is

The vibe inside is super-sultry, making this a great date-night spot as well.

always on the menu, and although the preparation varies, you can assume it's going to be delicious. Pictured is the tuna tartare with a watermelon jus, chunks of watermelon, Japanese ginger, radish, and cucumber. Pairs well with lighter cocktails!

THE RITTENHOUSE CRAWL

1. THE LOVE, **130 S. 18th St., Philadelphia, (215) 433-1555,** theloverestaurant.com

2. MAC MART, **104 S. 18th St., Philadelphia, (215) 444-6144,** macmartcart.com

3. HUDA, **32 S. 18th St., Philadelphia, (445) 544-8025,** hudaphl.com

4. METROPOLITAN BAKERY/CAFE, **262 S. 19th St., Philadelphia,** **(215) 545-6655, metropolitanbakery.com**

5. HARP & CROWN, **1525 Sansom St., Philadelphia, (215) 330-2800,** harpcrown.com

6. ABE FISHER, **1623 Sansom St., Philadelphia, (215) 867-0088,** abefisherphilly.com

7. MONK'S CAFE, **264 S. 16th St., Philadelphia, (215) 545-7005,** monkscafe.com

Rittenhouse

The heart of Philadelphia lies right in the center

One of Philly's most desirable neighborhoods, Rittenhouse extends far beyond just Rittenhouse Square, the city's famous park. Lining the park are amazing alfresco dining options. A few steps beyond it, a shopaholic's paradise. Throughout the famed shopping district, restaurants and bars serve up worldly cuisines. From a quick bite to a multicourse fine-dining experience, Rittenhouse is a neighborhood that truly has it all.

1

THE LOVE

Your tasty journey through Rittenhouse begins at THE LOVE, where you're sure to love the cozy atmosphere, friendly service, and upscale take on traditional dishes. The Love features seasonal American fare, meaning that the menu rotates according to what's fresh and in season, which means you can enjoy something different every time you go. While they serve lunch and dinner every day, on weekends you can catch a delicious brunch before making your way through the rest of the neighborhood.

Start with the cinnamon bun scones, which are the perfect cinnamon bun–scone hybrid. They're crunchy on the outside, soft on the inside, with ribbons of cinnamon goodness throughout. To take things over the top, they're topped with cream-cheese frosting and served with a side of whipped coffee butter, which tastes like a creamy latte and pairs perfectly with the scones. For your main event, try the Lemon Poppy Pancakes, which are super-special. The pancakes themselves are lightly lemon flavored and dotted with poppy seeds, and served with candied ginger syrup and sour cherry sauce. Forget standard pancakes with maple syrup—these are a truly elevated version of a comfort food classic. Sweet, tangy, fruity, and tart all at the same time, they'll have you wishing you could eat breakfast for every meal.

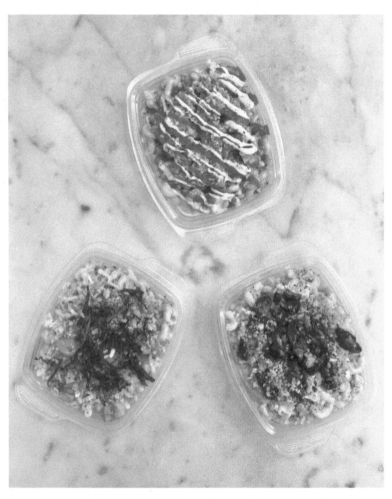

2 MAC MART

Your second stop of the day takes you to Philadelphia's beloved cheesy mecca, MAC MART. It originally began as a food truck, run by founder Marti Lieberman. The hot-pink truck served mac and cheese with various toppings at weddings, festivals, and night markets. It has since exploded into something much bigger, and Marti was able to open a bustling fast-casual storefront in the heart of the Rittenhouse neighborhood in 2016. From the kitschy pink decor to the enticing aroma of fresh cheesy goodness, this place has good vibes written all over it.

Each bowl at Mac Mart starts with a standard mac-and-cheese base that's anything but your standard mac and cheese. Mac Mart specializes in non-baked, seven-cheese mac and cheese made with a combination of mild cheeses that act as the perfect base for the extensive toppings menu that they offer. It's the perfect place to come with friends to sample a few different things, each of which is more delicious than the next. The Margherita Mac is topped with fresh mozzarella, tomato, basil, and a potato-chip panko crunch, and it's a delightful Italian twist on mac and cheese. Jalapeño Popper Mac kicks the base up a notch by infusing it with jalapeño oil for a nice kick, and it's topped with house-fried jalapeño popper dip and potato-chip panko crunch for a creamy, cheese, spicy, crunchy bite. Lastly, one of the most popular creations (for good reason) is In the Buff, which is the classic base topped with chunks of chicken tossed in buffalo sauce, a healthy smattering of buttermilk ranch, and the iconic panko and potato-chip crunch. As you finish off your last few bites of cheesy heaven, get ready for the next stop on your Rittenhouse food tour, which boasts some of the area's tastiest breads and slices.

3 HUDA

The former head chef at Abe Fisher (which you'll find later in this neighborhood crawl), Yehuda Sichel set out on his own when he opened Huda in Rittenhouse. Inspired by a love of sandwiches, this fast-casual spot, known for its house-made milk buns, is beloved by locals and visitors alike.

If you're visiting Huda for the first time, there are two things you need to try. First, a sandwich (duh). The Brisket Sandwich, with dijonnaise, garlic pickles, and onion is a personal favorite. It's salty, flavorful, and oh-so-tender, and it's made even better by the pillowy soft milk bun it's served on. Second, you need to try a sweet bun. Also house-made milk buns—the sweet buns feature a delicious filling and topping that make them a dessert to be reckoned with. While the toppings may change (concord grapes + mascarpone frosting, grapefruit, etc.), they're always a slam dunk.

4 METROPOLITAN BAKERY/CAFE

Stop no. 3 lands you at METROPOLITAN BAKERY/CAFE, a Philadelphia favorite, known for their exquisite breads and baked goods. Founded in 1993 by Wendy Smith Born and James Barrett, who met while working at White Dog Cafe (a stop in the University City Food Crawl), Metropolitan has grown to have four retail outlets, a cafe, and a busy online business. You can also find Metropolitan Bakery

goods served at some of Philadelphia's finest restaurants, and the bakery has truly turned into a Philly institution. In Rittenhouse they have an adorable cafe and bakery that not only sells their breads and pastries but makes outrageously good pizza, which is exactly what you're after.

Start your pizza party off with a classic Margherita pizza, which is made with Metropolitan's handmade dough and topped with roasted tomato, mozzarella, stracciatella, basil, oregano, and olive oil. Next, try some of their unique flavor combos, such as those in the Mushroom Pizza, which has garlic crema, fontina, mozzarella, taleggio, thyme, scallions, assorted mushrooms, and Parmesan. The Sausage Pizza comes topped with freshly made sausage, roasted tomato, fennel, red onion, fennel pollen, and caciocavallo, and makes for a great hearty option. They also frequently change up their special pies to mirror what's in season, so don't be afraid to try something out of your comfort zone! When it's made on Metropolitan dough, it's guaranteed to be good.

TIP

There's also a Metropolitan Bakery in Reading Terminal Market, where you can also grab a loaf/baked good to go!

5

HARP & CROWN

Maybe it's the high, lofty ceilings, maybe it's the gorgeous antiques lining the walls, or maybe it's the cool new-age yet vintage vibe. Whatever it is, HARP & CROWN is one of Philly's coolest restaurants, making it the perfect spot to spend happy hour in the City of Brotherly Love. Their happy hour features a $5 house cocktail, which is dealer's choice. Given Harp & Crown's extensive bar and knowledgeable bartenders, it's usually bound to be something good. You can also get a beer or a house wine for $5, so it's a great place to knock back a few drinks without racking up a crazy bar tab.

Michael Schulson and his wife, Nina, have a knack for taking near-forgotten spaces and transforming them. Harp & Crown is a perfect example of that—the duo completely renovated the space to create a fabulous restaurant with a bowling alley in it. The high ceilings, vintage wallpaper, leather club chairs, and natural colors paired with an innovative, modern menu bring together the charm of times past with the excitement of the present.

For some bites, the Whipped Ricotta is excellent. Served with just olive oil, sea salt, and some fresh bread, it's proof that simple can be best. The lamb meatballs, which are served with a delicious tangy yogurt sauce, are a perfect hearty bite that won't leave you overly full. For the main event, grab a daily seasonal pizza for just $5—you can't beat that deal. If you're looking to work off some of today's eats, grab a lane and enjoy a game of bowling with your frinds before heading off to the next stop for dinner.

6 ABE FISHER

The vibe at ABE FISHER is sultry, dark, and cozy. From the modern bar to the retro decor, it's a true "Old World meets New World" restaurant, and the menu reflects just that. Mike Solomonov (who has a few other hits in this book, such as Dizengoof, Zahav, K'Far Cafe, and Federal Donuts) hit a home run when he opened Abe Fisher in the Rittenhouse neighborhood. The restaurant serves a modern twist on Jewish classics and elevates them for a fine-dining experience.

The best way to enjoy Abe Fisher is to try a bit of everything. Start with the potato latke, served

TIP

Abe Fisher offers a prix fixe menu year-round, so it's the perfect place to step out of your comfort zone and try something new!

with applesauce and sour cream. It's a classic comfort food executed perfectly—the latke is crispy and flavorful, and the accompaniments add great taste and balance to the dish. Next, try the Pickled Mackerel, which is served with Bibb lettuce to create delicious, tangy lettuce wraps. The Veal Schnitzel Tacos are a must, and they're a fan favorite for good reason. Buttery anchovy mayo complements the perfectly crisped veal pieces, enrobed in a soft taco shell for an elevated taste with fun presentation. Lastly, this is not the place to skip on dessert. There's typically a seasonal dessert in addition to the menu staples (like the infamous Bacon & Egg Cream).

7 MONK'S CAFE

There's no better place to end your night in Rittenhouse than at MONK'S CAFE, a true Philly institution. Opened in April of 1997, this cozy neighborhood bistro began serving beers from around the world as well as food to complement them. Proprietors Tom Peters and Bernadette Roe have created more than just a restaurant—Monk's Cafe has become a community gathering place. Boasting literally hundreds of beers from global breweries large and small, Monk's Cafe has not only been the first place where many breweries have debuted beers, but it's also the place where thousands of people have found their (new) favorite beers.

If you're visiting, you must start with a glass of Monk's Cafe Flemish Sour Ale. It's the restaurant's own private label, brewed for them in Belgium by the family-owned Van Steenberge brewery. It's red in color, somewhat fruity, malty, and has a bit of sourness that makes it the perfect palate cleanser between bites. In addition to an outrageous beer selection, Monk's is also known for their *cuisine à la bière*, aka food to pair with your beer. Start with the beet hummus, which is as tasty as it is vibrant and bright. Next, the Duck Salad, which is served with goat cheese, spicy walnuts, and Craisins, is the perfect light bite after a day of eating. Lastly, Monk's Cafe is known for their mussels, so it would essentially be a crime in Philadelphia to leave without trying some. You can get them cooked any which way you'd like, from Thai curry to smoked to cheesy, but the Mexicano is a perfect

Monk's Cafe knows its Belgians. Co-founder Tom Peters is a Knight of the Belgian Mashstaff, the ancient order of Belgian brewers, in recognition of his work in introducing Belgian beer to America. Monk's Cafe was also the first place in the world outside of Belgium to serve Chimay on draft, and it has been named an official Ambassadeur Orval for twelve consecutive years—a recognition by the Abbey that Orval Trappist Ale is optimally stored, served, and represented.

testament to Monk's Cafe. The mussels are stewed in Monk's Cafe Flemish Sour Ale, served with lime, peppers, onions, jalapeños, cilantro, and Monk's famous pomme frites (crispy fries). It's the perfect food to snack on while you try some new beers and make some new memories in Philadelphia.

THE GRADUATE HOSPITAL CRAWL

1. **PORCOS PORCHETTERIA AND SMALL OVEN PASTRY SHOP, 2204 Washington Ave., Philadelphia, (215) 545-2939, smallovencafe.com**

2. **DOCK STREET BREWERY SOUTH, 2118 Washington Ave., Philadelphia, (215) 337-3103, dockstreetbeer.com**

3. **SALLY, 2229 Spruce St., Philadelphia, (267) 773-7178, sallyphl.com**

4. **TRATTORIA CARINA, 2201 Spruce St., Philadelphia, (215) 732-5818, trattoriacarina.com**

5. **SOUTHGATE, 1801 Lombard St., Philadelphia, (215) 560-8443, southgatephilly.com**

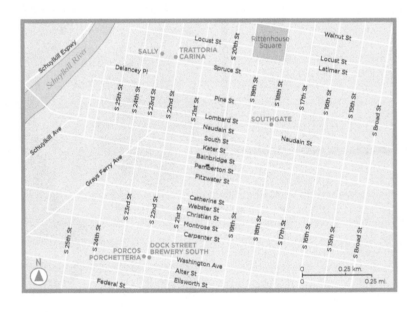

Graduate Hospital

Quintessential neighborhood charm

South of Rittenhouse, Graduate Hospital was originally named for a large medical institution which is no longer there. Rather, the neighborhood has established itself as a sought-after place that perfectly melds a downtown feel with neighborhood charm. Family friendly and dotted with local shops, bars, and restaurants, it's an area that boasts amazing food and drink in a laid-back atmosphere. From pizza to pasta to kimchi fries and seasonal beers, you're in for a variety of culinary delights.

1

PORCOS PORCHETTERIA AND SMALL OVEN PASTRY SHOP

This place is the definition of a "two for one" kind of deal. This little storefront is home to not one but two of Philly's tastiest spots. Under the helm of Chef Chad Durkin, this fast-casual walk-up concept is a neighborhood staple. On one side, PORCOS PORCHETTERIA serves all-natural (read: no antibiotics, humanely raised, locally sourced) pork-focused dishes. Here, you need to grab a breakfast sandwich with house-made porchetta on it, as there's really no better way to start your day. It's the perfect combination of rich and salty, with the pork adding great texture. It's a great way to start a day of eating, and you can totally take it to go. But, before you go—don't forget to grab something sweet! Right next door, SMALL OVEN PASTRY SHOP is cranking out beautiful, sophisticated baked goods. From macarons to s'mores bars to cookies and more, this place is sure to satisfy even the most discerning sweet tooth.

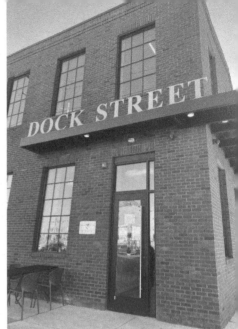

DOCK STREET BREWERY SOUTH

Is it ever too early for a drink? What better way to break up a day of eating than with a refreshing beverage (and maybe another snack, honestly) at DOCK STREET BREWERY SOUTH. Just a few steps from Porcos and Small Oven, this neighborhood watering hole boasts good beers and good vibes. One of Philly's first craft breweries, Dock Street Brewery has been a Philly staple since 1985. Grab a seasonal beer, get a charcuterie board for snacking, and stay a while. They're constantly adding new beers to their draft list, and they make a mean cocktail (with house-made syrups and Pennsylvania local spirits). Dock Street also offers wood-fired pizzas, shareables, and more—great for groups and great for sharing! Nosh away while you hydrate (ha, get it) in preparation for a delicious day of eating!

3

SALLY

A relatively new addition to the neighborhood, opening in 2020, SALLY came in swinging. A simple menu—sourdough pizzas, small plates, and natural wines, but this place absolutely nails every single thing on there. The menu may seem unassuming, with many items having super-simple names, though the dishes themselves are anything but. Ingredients are intricately paired to create truly unique, delicious flavor combinations that

you won't find anywhere else. The menu changes every few months, so you're in for a surprise whenever you go. If it's on the menu, the house-made ricotta is delicate, light, and insanely good, paired with a toasted sourdough. The oysters and anchovies are perfect salty light bites to kick off a tasty meal as well. Try some of their veggie dishes, like the beets, alongside a pizza (which you MUST get). The Soppressata Pizza with pepper relish is a personal favorite, and the Mushroom and Egg Pizza is creamy, rich, and delightful. Wash it all down with a glass of natural wine before you continue to eat your way through this delicious neighborhood.

4 TRATTORIA CARINA

TRATTORIA CARINA is a casual neighborhood Italian restaurant from the same minds behind Pub & Kitchen (another neighborhood fave). At just thirty-two seats, this little spot is cozy, charming, and the food is downright delicious. The menu changes seasonally but is always focused on homemade pastas and Italian favorites, so no matter when you go, you're sure to have a memorable meal.

Start with their house-made meatballs, which are tender,

juicy, and served with whipped ricotta. Next, any vegetable dish makes the perfect light bite before the main event (their roasted + pickled carrots and their beets with ricotta and pistachio are a personal favorite). For your main, the chicken Parmesan is some of my favorite in the city. Perfectly fried, the chicken is juicy, the breading is flavorful, and it's all topped in a tasty pomodoro sauce and *alllll* the melted buffalo mozzarella. The cacio e pepe is a classic done well, and the gemelli with pistachio pesto is flavorful but light—the perfect bite!

End your meal on a sweet note with any of Trattoria Carina's homemade desserts. Their tiramisu is excellent, and they typically have a dessert special if you're looking to try something new!

5

SOUTHGATE

The perfect place to end the night, SOUTHGATE is equal parts delicious and cool. Southgate is all about taking classic dishes and giving them a Korean flair, in a laid-back space that's perfect for hanging out. Grab some small plates, an inventive cocktail, and stay a while.

First, grab a cocktail made with soju, a Korean liquor distilled from sweet potatoes and rice. It has a super-interesting flavor profile, and Southgate has their own tasty flavor infusions. You can get it on its own or in a cocktail, like the Kkachi, made with grapefruit soju, tequila, Lillet, Aperol, and lime.

For bites, try the pork dumplings (steamed or fried), which are tender, juicy, and full of flavor. Next, get the Kimchi Fries, which are covered in

bacon, onions, cheese, and a tangy vinaigrette—a perfect example of the epic Korean fusion that Southgate does so well. The Korean Fried Chicken is insanely tasty—sweet, spicy, and perfectly crispy. If you're looking for something more substantial, end your night with their Kimchi Cheeseburger—which features a bulgogi beef patty, Kewpie mayo, perilla leaf, and it's topped with kimchi, bacon, and cheese. It's a creamy, spicy, tangy flavor combination that you won't find in another burger!

THE SOUTH PHILLY/EAST PASSYUNK CRAWL

1. THE DUTCH, **1527 S. 4th St.**, Philadelphia, **(215) 755-5600,** thedutchphilly.com

2. MIKE'S BBQ, **1703 S. 11th St.**, Philadelphia, **(267) 831-2040,** mikesbbqphilly.com

3. ESSEN BAKERY, **1437 E. Passyunk Ave.**, Philadelphia, **(215) 271-2299,** essenbakery.com

4. STARGAZY, **1838 E. Passyunk Ave.**, Philadelphia, **(215) 309-2761,** facebook.com/StargazyPhilly

5. BING BING DIM SUM, **1648 E. Passyunk Ave.**, Philadelphia, **(215) 279-7702, bingbingdimsum.com**

6. ITV (IN THE VALLEY), **1615 E. Passyunk Ave.**, Philadelphia, **(267) 858-0669, itvphilly.com**

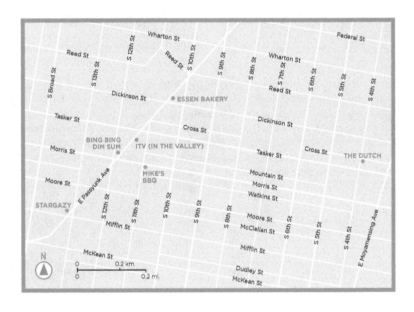

South Philly/East Passyunk

More than just cheesesteaks

Passyunk Avenue intersects the typical grid design of Philadelphia, slicing right through South Philly. The avenue itself is fun and vibrant, from the shops to restaurants and cafes. Here, you can find anything from exotic plants to vintage clothing to worldly cuisine, and it even landed a spot on *Food and Wine*'s list of Ten Best Foodie Streets in America. There's a reason it's a favorite spot for locals (especially those of the foodie persuasion). Just beyond the avenue you can find a perfect mesh of old-world charm and new energy, making it a perfect place to spend a day exploring.

1

THE DUTCH

Your day starts at THE DUTCH, which is, you guessed it, a Dutch-inspired eatery. Started by Joncarl Lachman (the mind behind East Passyunk's Noord) and Lee Styer (owner of Fond), The Dutch strictly serves breakfast/brunch/lunch seven days a week, from 8 a.m. to 3 p.m. Inspired by Styer's Pennsylvania Dutch background and French technique plus Lachman's Dutch background, the menu pulls from both genres, creating an eclectic mix of flavors that are sure to delight.

Kick things off with the Savory Dutch Baby, which is a cast iron-cooked pancake with smoked sausage, scallions, and finished with powdered sugar. It's smoky, hearty, and slightly sweet, if you can't decide between salty or sweet for breakfast. If you're feeling more savory, the Savory Scallion Waffle with Creamed Chipped Beef is a slam dunk. It's creamy and rich, served on a waffle with just the right amount of tang from the scallions. If you're more into sweet breakfast, get the Ana Banana Pancakes, which are sweet pancakes served with bananas, blueberries, whipped cream, and powdered sugar—a classic. If you're still in the mood for something savory, though, then you're in luck, because our next stop takes us to one of Philly's best BBQ spots.

2 MIKE'S BBQ

MIKE'S BBQ is a no-frills BBQ joint serving everything from crispy pork belly to ribs to cheesesteaks (and all the delicious sides that go along with them), and most days they're lucky if they can make it until 6 p.m. before selling out. Yeah, it's that good. Michael Strauss, the man behind the meat, spent years making his style of BBQ for friends and family, apprenticing along the way. Once he had garnered enough experience, he drove down to Georgia and got himself a Lang Smoker, which is an old school–style stick smoker, and opened up Mike's BBQ on 11th Street.

Currently there are no walk-ins, and orders must be placed online. Start with some classics—a full rack of ribs, dry rubbed and smoked until they're falling off the bone, and expertly prepared Lancaster Chicken Wings. Both are tender, juicy, and so flavorful that you really don't need sauce. The Brisket Cheesesteak is also a must-try—you are in Philly, after all. The sandwich starts with tender brisket, elevated by a healthy dose of fried onions and Cooper Sharp Whiz, for a Philly cheesesteak that's anything but ordinary.

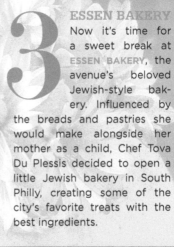

3

ESSEN BAKERY

Now it's time for a sweet break at **ESSEN BAKERY**, the avenue's beloved Jewish-style bakery. Influenced by the breads and pastries she would make alongside her mother as a child, Chef Tova Du Plessis decided to open a little Jewish bakery in South Philly, creating some of the city's favorite treats with the best ingredients.

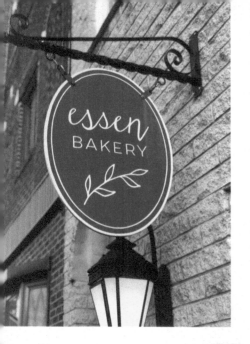

This is definitely one of those places where it's hard to recommend something, since pretty much everything is good. The best thing you can do is check out the pastry case when you get here, take an inventory of what's available (they sell out pretty fast), and then get one (or two) of everything. If the chocolate halva babka is available, get it. Get a slice if you have self-control and grab a loaf if not. It's buttery, chocolatey, and indulgent—a perfect rendition of a Jewish classic. Same goes for the chocolate rugelach, which are bite-sized chocolate pastries that are small enough that you can eat three ... or five ... without worry. The black-and-white cookie is another classic that's executed perfectly, and they even have a variety of flavors (though you can't go wrong with a classic). There is also an assortment of fruity pastries, challah flavors, bagels, and more that rotate regularly, which just gives you a reason to come back!

4

STARGAZY

Chef Sam Jacobson is bringing a taste of London to Philly with his British bakery STARGAZY. In England savory pies are a low-cost, savory, delicious sustenance option, typically served with mashed potatoes and parsley sauce. They're often accompanied by jellied eels (yes, real eels, like from the ocean), which Jacobsen carries as well. However, Stargazy is more than just a pie shop—it's a true taste of England in Philadelphia.

The first thing you'll notice is that Stargazy carries an extensive array of British goodies, from chips to candies and more. The second thing you'll notice is the pastry case, which is likely stocked with some things you've never seen before. This is the fun part. Start off savory, with a classic savory pie, mash, and some jellied eels (when in London, right?).

Next, have a Sausage Roll, which is like a pig in a blanket's cooler, more grown-up cousin. Then, try a Bedfordshire Clanger, which is a revelation in pie. It's a long pastry that has a savory filling on one end and a sweet filling on the other. It's literally a meal and dessert in one (and the part where savory meets sweet in the middle is oh so satisfying). Lastly, if there are Millionaire Bars available, get one. Heck, get two. It's a buttery shortbread base topped with homemade caramel, chocolate, and sea salt, and it fully warrants the Millionaire title—it'll have you feeling like you just struck dessert gold.

5

BING BING DIM SUM

BING BING DIM SUM oozes cool, from the funky graffiti on the walls to the neon string lights to the patrons that inhabit it. Bing Bing specializes in Chinese plates with a Jewish twist, meaning you literally can't find this stuff elsewhere. Started by dudes from Philly (who also own Cheu Fishtown, nunu, and Cheu

Noodle Bar, all of which serve Asian-inspired cuisine), Shawn Darragh and Ben Puchowitz focus less on tradition and more on making food they'd want to eat themselves (and we're all happily along for the ride).

This is the perfect place to split a bunch of plates with a group. Start with the Spicy Sichuan Cucumbers, which are tossed in ma la vinegar with tofu and watercress. They're crunchy, spicy, and slightly sweet, making them the perfect starter. Next, the Cheesesteak Bao is about as Philly as it gets. It's a soft, pillowy bao stuffed with Cooper Sharp cheese, long hots, and

chopped steak and tastes like a Philly cheesesteak with a twist. The Scarlet Dumplings, known for their bright-red color, are served with Swiss chard, tofu, and crispy garlic for a flavor that's light yet bold. Don't skip the Caterpillar Bread—a sweet bread filled with barbecued pork, caramelized honey, and sesame, bursting with sweet, tangy flavor. Lastly, for something more filling, try the Caramel Pork Shank. The pork is fall-off-the-bone tender, with a delicious sweetness to it. It's complemented by tangy Vietnamese pickles and sambal and served with steamed buns so you can make little sandwiches. So go ahead, play with your food.

6   ITV (IN THE VALLEY)

The perfect spot to wrap up your food tour is none other than cozy cocktail bar ITV (which stands for In the Valley). From the mastermind behind Philly favorites such as Royal Boucherie (find it in the Old City Crawl) and Laurel comes a bar that chef-owner Nicholas Elmi has dubbed French-inspired cuisine meets an extensive wine list and thoughtfully curated, seasonally inspired cocktails. What's awesome about ITV is that you can munch on house-made pork chips (think pork rinds but better) and down a beer, or you can get champagne and caviar service—you really can have it all here.

The menu is mostly small bites, which pair perfectly with the various cocktail, wine, and beer options. The Goose Fat Biscuit with Honey Chive Butter is excellent—crunchy on the outside, soft and fluffy on the inside.

The butter is sweet, salty, and indulgent, making for a seriously killer bar snack. The Potato Pancakes with Applesauce and Sour Cream are as good as Bubbie used to make—crispy, savory, and perfectly complemented by the sweet applesauce and sour cream. As far as drinks go, you really can't go wrong here. With a fifty-bottle wine list, beers to boot, and cocktails that change with the season, you have something for everyone. As far as standard cocktails go, the Show Me Your Bloobies, made with Wild Turkey 101 Rye, cognac, St-Germain, Blueberry Shrub, and lemon, is fruity, tart, and lightly sweet. If you happen to hit ITV around the holidays, it transforms into a festive wonderland, and the drinks all get a fun, festive twist. So enjoy some snacks, try a drink outside of your comfort zone, and hang out like a local on Passyunk Ave.

BONUS CRAWL! SOUTH PHILLY CHEESESTEAK

1. PAT'S KING OF STEAKS, 1237 E. Passyunk Ave., Philadelphia, (215) 468-1546, patskingofsteaks.com

2. GENO'S STEAKS, 1219 S. 9th St., Philadelphia, (215) 389-0659, genosteaks.com

3. ISHKABIBBLE'S, 337 South St., Philadelphia, (215) 923-4337, philacheesesteak.com

4. JIM'S STEAKS, 400 South St., Philadelphia, (215) 928-1911, jimssteaks.com

5. WOODROW'S SANDWICH SHOP, 630 South St., Philadelphia, (215) 470-3559, woodrowsandwich.com

Bonus Crawl!
South Philly Cheesesteak

If there's one thing Philly is known for, it's cheesesteaks. Many will try to replicate them, but there's ultimately nothing like an iconic Philly cheesesteak eaten in Philly (bonus points if you eat it in an Eagles jersey with the *Fresh Prince of Bel Air* theme song playing). Wit, wit-out, cheesy, beefy, or made with chicken or elevated ingredients like truffle—no matter how you order it, just be sure you don't leave Philly without trying at least one of these iconic South Philly steaks.

1

PAT'S KING OF STEAKS

It's only right that this crawl begins with the self-proclaimed inventor of the Philly cheesesteak, **PAT'S KING OF STEAKS**. Founded by Pat Olivieri in 1930, the institution is still owned and run by the Olivieri family. Pat's

HOW TO ORDER AT PAT'S

Pat's is typically bustling and the line moves fast, so have your order ready to go by the time you make it to the front.

First, decide if you want it *wit* (with onions) or *witout* (no onions).

Next, decide if you want provolone, American cheese, or Cheez Whiz, or you can get it plain or pizza-steak style.

Lastly, get your cash out—Pat's is cash only. You grab your steak at the first window, and then order drinks/fries at the second window.

has just one location, remaining open 24/7 to satisfy Philly's cheesesteak cravings.

To truly experience Pat's, you have to go for a classic cheesesteak. Meat, onions, cheese, and bread are really all it takes to create a mouthwatering sandwich, just as Pat himself made over ninety years ago. From the soft bread to freshly cooked steak, tangy onions, and creamy cheese, it's Philly in a bite.

Conveniently, your next stop is across the street, and poses an interesting rivalry in the city.

2

GENO'S STEAKS

If you're looking for Philly's tastiest rivalry, you've found it. "Pat's or Geno's?" is a polarizing topic in the city, and given that they're across the street from each other, you get to decide for yourself. Similar to Pat's, GENO'S is a Philly institution. Joey Vento opened Geno's in 1966, with two boxes of steaks and $6 in his pocket. Joey learned the ropes working in his family's steak shop in the 1940s, so he decided to stick with what he knew—steaks. People flocked to the shop, and the business grew so much that when Joey's son was born in 1971, he named him Geno. Since Joey's passing in 2011, Geno continues to run the shop just as his father would have wanted.

To properly compare this cheesesteak to the previous one, it's only right that you order another classic cheesesteak (this spot is also cash only and open 24/7). If, however, you're feeling adventurous, they offer plenty of options—with mushrooms, peppers, fried tomatoes, and more. As you finish scarfing down your sandwich, get ready for a nice walk (gotta walk off those steaks to eat more steaks!) to our next stop.

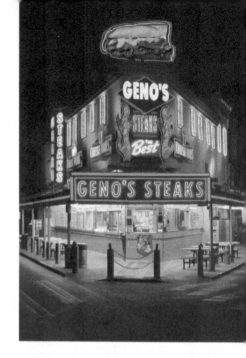

3 ISHKABIBBLE'S

Since 1979 ISHKABIBBLE'S has been satisfying the cheesesteak cravings of locals and tourists alike. However, their claim to fame is actually the chicken cheesesteak, as they're the proclaimed originator of it. This spot is a local favorite because of the delicious sandwiches and the Gremlin drink, which is a lemonade and grape juice drink that pairs great with a salty, savory sandwich.

At Ishkabibble's you have to try the chicken cheesesteak. They're all made-to-order, with juicy chicken, onions, peppers, and ooey-gooey cheese (you have your choice of cheese). The chicken cheesesteak is the perfect departure from the traditional cheesesteaks you've been scarfing down, but the chicken is so flavorful that you won't miss beef. But in case you do, you'll be happy about the next stop.

4

JIM'S STEAKS

Just across the street from Ishkabibble's, you'll see the iconic black-and-white sign that means one thing: You're at JIM'S STEAKS. The original Jim's Steaks was opened in West Philadelphia on 62nd Street in 1939, where it still operates to this day. In 1976 Jim's expanded to South Street, which is where you find yourself today. The Art Deco style of the shop is basically a Philly landmark, and the family traditions behind each and every cheesesteak are beloved by both those who visit this city and those who live in it.

Jim's is another place to try a classic—chopped steak, Cheez Whiz, and all the onions. This cheesesteak is an ooey-gooey, delicious mess, made fresh to order and bursting with real Philly flavor. Each bite is a salty, cheesy, almost buttery delight that you're sure to remember.

5 WOODROW'S SANDWICH SHOP

WOODROW'S specializes in all things sandwich, from a Cubano to a Coffee BBQ Brisket Sandwich. While not exclusively in the cheesesteak biz, they make one of the best, and it happens to be right along the route of this crawl.

The Woodrow's Whiz Wit is pretty much legendary among Philadelphians, as it's a gourmet twist on a classic. The sandwich starts with shaved rib eye and is topped with caramelized onions, a cherry pepper mayo, and truffle whiz. Yes, you read that right—truffle whiz. It makes all the difference, as it gives this cheesesteak a depth of flavor while still being reminiscent of a classic cheesesteak. The caramelized onions add a hint of sweetness, the mayo has a distinct pepper flavor, and the truffle whiz has the delightfully earthy notes of truffle melded with the creamy, familiar flavor and texture of Cheez Whiz. It's a slam dunk, and the perfect place to end your cheesesteak tour of Philadelphia. So, which was your favorite?

BONUS CRAWL! SOUTH PHILLY PIZZA

1. EMMY SQUARED, Queen Village, 632 S. 5th St., Philadelphia, (267) 551-3669, emmysquaredpizza.com

2. NOMAD PIZZA, 611 S. 7th St., Philadelphia, (215) 238-0900, nomadpizzaco.com

3. ANGELO'S PIZZERIA SOUTH PHILLY, 736 S. 9th St., Philadelphia, (215) 922-0000, angelospizzeriasouthphiladelphia.com

4. SANTUCCI'S ORIGINAL SQUARE PIZZA, 901 S. 10th St., Philadelphia, (215) 825-5304, santuccispizza.com

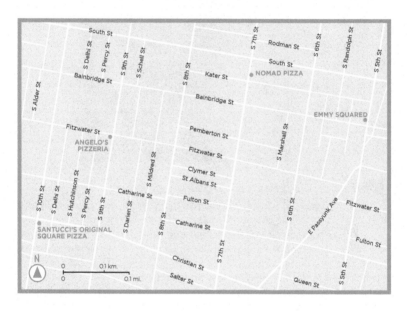

Bonus Crawl! South Philly Pizza

Philadelphia is a city that takes its pizza seriously, and the pizza shops all over the city prove that. No two pizza places are alike, each honing their craft and putting passion into their product. While Philly has amazing pizza all over, there are a few gems in South Philadelphia that are worth checking out, and they happen to make for a perfect neighborhood crawl. So, throw on your eating pants and get ready to go to Pizza Paradise.

1 EMMY SQUARED

Originally hailing from New York, EMMY SQUARED landed in Philadelphia in late 2019 and was instantly loved by locals. Part of the Pizza Loves Emily family of restaurants, co-founded by Emily Hyland and executive chef Matthew Hyland, Emmy Squared focuses on quality ingredients, unique toppings, and making a killer Detroit-style pizza.

What is Detroit-style pizza, you ask? It's marked by its square shape, pillowy dough, crispy bottom, stripes of sauce, and a signature cheese crust. The perfect pizza to try here is one that's simple but really lets the style shine—the Margherita. It's unlike any other Margherita pizza you've had, as it's topped with fresh burrata and basil, making for a much creamier, more decadent bite than a typical Margherita pie. Each bite is magical, moving from crispy to soft to bursting with flavor. You'll quickly understand why Emmy Squared

TIP

Though this is a pizza crawl, people go crazy for the Le Big Matt, which is the restaurant's famed double-stack burger.

has garnered such a cult following. If you're looking for something to pair with your pie, try an order of waffle fries with chopped cheese. The fries come loaded with grass-fed chopped beef, red onion, bell pepper, pickles, and a smoky queso sauce that will have you licking the plate clean.

Enjoy your bites in Emmy's gorgeous space, which is large, sleek, and modern, making it an awesome spot for a group or a celebration. What's a party without pizza, anyway?

2 NOMAD PIZZA

In 2007 NOMAD PIZZA was born out of the back of an old REO Speedwagon. The mobile pizzeria catered parties throughout the Jersey area, and people were constantly asking where they could pick up Nomad's unique pizzas. The original Nomad opened in New Jersey, followed by a location in Philadelphia, which has become a pizza mainstay in the city. Focusing on Neapolitan-style and Roman-style pizza, Nomad prides themselves on using quality ingredients to create unique flavor combinations that keep people coming back for more.

Nomad is doing things right, using a dough that's homemade with minimal ingredients and firing their pizzas in a wood oven at 850 degrees, ensuring a crispy, crunchy crust but deliciously chewy, soft center for every pie. When you visit, start with the Pesto Pizza, which is topped with fresh mozzarella, cherry tomatoes, and roasted red pepper. It's vegetarian yet satisfying, and the flavors of the tomato and pepper really shine through. The Guanciale Pizza is also excellent, topped with spinach, guanciale (pork), shredded mozzarella, Parmesan, black pepper, garlic, and fig jam. It's salty and sweet, savory yet light, and is super-unique and perfectly representative of what Nomad does best—simple, quick pizza that's fresh and delicious.

3 ANGELO'S PIZZERIA SOUTH PHILLY

ANGELO'S is cash only. They don't do slices, meaning you have to get a whole pie, which is the opposite of a problem, as it's likely to be some of the most delicious pizza to grace your taste buds.

A pizza shop has to be pretty confident to open up a no-call-ahead, wait-for-your-whole-pie operation in the heart of the Italian Market, but Angelo's backs it up with incredible pizza. One of the most beloved pies is the Upside Down Jawn (it doesn't get more Philly), which is a thick-crust square-pan pizza with the sauce on top of the cheese. Perfectly chewy crust meets super-fresh ingredients for insanely satisfying taste in every bite. For something circular (beauty comes in all shapes), try the Trenton, which is made with whole-milk mozzarella, extra-virgin olive oil,

TIP

If you're a follower of *Barstool Sports'* One Bite Pizza Reviews, Barstool president Dave Portnoy came to Angelo's in November of 2019 and declared it the best pizza in Philadelphia. On his 1–10 rating scale, it scored a 9.1.

oregano, pecorino Romano, and dolloped with fresh ground tomatoes. Add pepperoni to kick this pizza up a notch, and get whisked away into pizza heaven. From the perfectly crispy crust to the rich mozzarella to the dollops of sweet tomato, it's everything you love about a classic pie done better. You also have the option to create your own pie here, starting with a tomato, white, or cheese base, and adding toppings like long hots, marinated artichokes, salami, sauce, prosciutto, and more. Go nuts and create your dream pizza, and let Angelo's make your dreams a reality.

4 SANTUCCI'S ORIGINAL SQUARE PIZZA

Founded by the late Joseph and Philomena Santucci, SANTUCCI'S has been slinging some of Philly's favorite pizza for over sixty years. In 1959 the Santuccis opened up shop on "O" Street in Juniata Park and began serving their family recipe for pizza, which was made in a square pan and served with the sauce on top of the cheese. Unconventional? Yes. Delicious? Absolutely. Now in its third generation of ownership, Santucci's has expanded throughout Philadelphia and South Jersey, providing patrons with brunch, lunch, and dinner, all while maintaining their commitment to their original family recipe.

It goes without saying that you must try a slice of Santucci's Square Pie. It's as simple as it gets—good dough, mozzarella, and pizza sauce on top—but don't let the simplicity fool you. The crust has the perfect consistency and is complemented by the mild taste of the cheese, finished with a wonderfully sweet tomato sauce—it's a downright addicting slice (which is probably why most people just get a whole pie). Though they're known for pizza, don't overlook the rest of Santucci's menu—from salads to sandwiches to pastas, they have an extensive offering of Italian favorites. Consider grabbing a Smoked Turkey Sandwich (a personal favorite) while you and your crew argue over which pizza from today's crawl was the best one.

THE UNIVERSITY CITY CRAWL

1. SCHMEAR IT, **3601 Market St. #5**, Philadelphia, (215) 792-3892, schmearit.com

2. SABRINA'S CAFE, **227 N. 34th St.**, Philadelphia, (215) 222-1022, sabrinascafe.com

3. WALNUT STREET CAFE, **2929 Walnut St.**, Philadelphia, (215) 867-8067, walnutstreetcafe.com

4. HAN DYNASTY, **3711 Market St.**, Philadelphia, (215) 222-3711, handynasty.net

5. WHITE DOG CAFE, **3420 Sansom St.**, Philadelphia, (215) 386-9224, whitedog.com

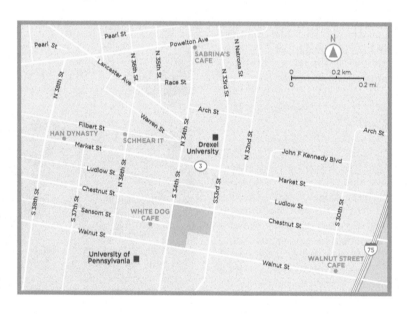

University City

In West Philadelphia, born and raised

University City gets its name from the multiple universities that share turf here. The University of Pennsylvania, Drexel University, University of the Sciences, and the Restaurant School at Walnut Hill College all reside in the same part of Philadelphia, creating a bustling part of town that's rich in culture, art, and, of course, food. This part of West Philadelphia has thrived due to the partnerships of anchor institutions, dedicated residents, and the local businesses that choose to open up shop here.

1 SCHMEAR IT

SCHMEAR IT's value proposition is pretty simple: Eat good bagels and do some good in the process. That's really what founder Dave Fine set out to do when he opened Philly's first all-bagel food truck that specializes in custom-crafted schmears and doing social good. The food truck was such a success that Dave ended up opening a brick-and-mortar store at 36th and Market, which is where this food crawl starts—with some good bagels that you can feel good about. Each month Schmear It features a Philadelphia-local cause to which a portion of sales will be donated, so you can really feel good about your purchase.

Start things off savory with the Loxsmith Bagel, which features a schmear that has lox, scallions, tomatoes, and cucumbers mixed right in, for a really unique take on a classic bagel combo. Next, get an egg sandwich (and definitely throw a hash brown on it for good measure if the option is available). Lastly, try a sweet bagel like the S'mores. Start with a chocolate-chip bagel, which will come loaded with cream cheese that's been expertly blended with Marshmallow Fluff, graham crackers, and chocolate chips. Who says you can't have dessert for breakfast?

TIP

Schmear It lets you order ahead if you're in a rush, and they have a dedicated gluten-free toaster!

2 SABRINA'S CAFE

The owners of Sabrina's sought to create a friendly, inviting space that served comforting food with a twist, all at a price that people could afford, and so SABRINA'S CAFE was born. Now, with five locations in Philadelphia and a consistently full house, that vision has come true.

Sabrina's is most well known in the city for their delicious breakfast and brunch menu, which is what you're after when you visit. Note that the menus change seasonally and vary by location, so you'll want to get whatever appeals to you at that moment in time, but allow me to make some suggestions. First off, if you can get an order of Polenta Fries, do it, because they'll make you forget all about regular potato fries as you get lost in their creamy yet thick texture and delightful flavor. Next, try an omelet or a hash dish (like the Ultimate Mexi Scramble with pepper jack cheese, peppers, tomatoes, and onions). Lastly, go for whatever the French toast special is (or get the Challah French Toast if you're not feeling adventurous). Sabrina's does a beautiful French toast on fluffy brioche bread, stuffed with everything you could imagine. The one pictured was a special that featured Oreo cookies, mascarpone, coconut cream cheese filling, a caramelized apple raisin syrup, and a mint chocolate drizzle—yeah, Sabrina's went there. Enjoy some coffee, tea, and good conversation in Sabrina's super-inviting space before heading on to your next stop for some lunch.

3 WALNUT STREET CAFE

I'm willing to bet that this will be one of the prettiest restaurants you've been in. Designed by a renowned firm out of New York, WALNUT STREET CAFE has a modern, chic aesthetic that heightens the overall experience as you work your way through a menu of New American fare, coffees, and cocktails.

Start off with a delicious cinnamon bun, paired with a strong cup of coffee, and take in the light, airy atmosphere. It's the perfect way to ease into a great meal here. Then, start off with a house-made soda and a farro salad, which is topped with butternut squash and dressed in a cider-truffle vinaigrette that's super-flavorful. Next, you must try a lobster roll, which comes elegantly plated on a bed of kettle potato chips. The fresh, poached lobster pairs beautifully with the buttery potato roll for a marvelous sandwich. Don't leave without trying Walnut Street Cafe's cheeseburger either, which is simple yet elegant and perfectly embodies the restaurant. The patty is topped with Wisconsin cheddar and caramelized onions, for a sweet, creamy, savory bite, and it's served with thin-cut fries. As you wrap up your meal, don't be afraid to linger over another cafe beverage or a specialty pastry (they have rotating scone options)—it's a super-inviting, aesthetically pleasing space full of friendly waitstaff, and it's an excellent addition to the University City neighborhood. Now, get ready to take your taste buds on a trip halfway around the world as you make your way to your next stop.

4 HAN DYNASTY

HAN DYNASTY offers quality, authentic Szechuan cuisine throughout the Philadelphia area, with locations in University City, Manayunk, and Old City, as well as additional locations in Pennsylvania and New York. Dishes are served family-style with an emphasis on choice—choice of sauce and choice of spice (1 being mild and 10 being a five-alarm fire).

Start with a lighter appetizer, like the spicy crispy cucumbers. They're basking in a glorious sauce that's a hint sweet and a stronger hint spicy and are the perfect snack food that's flavor-packed without being overly filling. Next, try an order of chicken fried dumplings, which are crispy on the outside yet tender and flavorful on the inside. For the main course, you have your choice of protein, sauce, and spice level. The Garlic Sauce Style Chicken is an excellent choice that's mild in spice but still has a nice kick. The chicken is cut into thin strips and stir-fried with garlic, ginger, bamboo, wood ear mushrooms, and bell peppers, finished in a sweet, sour, and spicy garlic sauce. Scoop some of the chicken over freshly made white rice and enjoy!

As you wrap up your meal, get ready for a culinary journey around the world at your next stop.

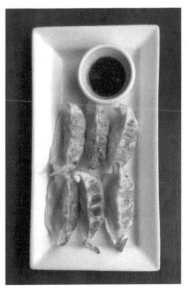

5 WHITE DOG CAFE

Judy Wicks opened WHITE DOG CAFE in January of 1983 in three connecting Victorian brownstones in University City. Her background in social activism made her popular with the locals, who began to flock to White Dog for its environmentally sustainable, community-engaged model. To this day, White Dog Cafe sources a vast majority of their ingredients from local farms, rotates menus to reflect what's in season, and employs renewable energy and sustainable initiatives in the restaurant.

As you enter the gorgeous space that is White Dog Cafe, you'll likely notice dogs—lots of them. From the door handles to the decor, this place is a dog lover's paradise. Luckily, it's great for food lovers too, as the restaurant consistently pushes the envelope of farm-to-table comfort food.

Note: Given that the menu changes seasonally, what you see in this book may not be what's on the menu at the time of your visit (though, there may be a variation of it). You can always ask the waitstaff for a suggestion!

Start your meal with the smoked salmon rillettes, which are delicious dollops of a smoked salmon mixture served alongside toasted pumpernickel bread, capers, radishes, and cornichons. Next, a bowl of Kennett Square Mushroom Soup is in order. It's served with a truffle crème fraîche and chives for a bowl of soup that's creamy, hearty, and bursting with mushroom flavor. Follow that with some butternut squash ravioli, served

with roasted apples, pickled fennel, candied pecan crunch, and a Pennsylvania Maple Cream sauce. It's a dish that's sweet yet balanced, full of flavor, and tastes how a hug feels. For entrees, start with the duck breast, pictured here served over a pumpkin polenta, alongside charred cipollini onions with a pomegranate agrodolce. The smokey duck pairs beautifully with the creamy polenta, tangy onions, and sweet sauce. Lastly, the lamb shank is exquisite (take it from someone who typically avoids lamb and basically licked the plate clean). The shank is served in a Szechuan peppercorn BBQ glaze over pillowy macadamia nut rice, with an Asian kohlrabi slaw. It's like a Chinese spin on a gourmet cut of lamb, and perfectly embodies what White Dog does best—transform local ingredients into something truly magical.

BONUS CRAWL! READING TERMINAL MARKET
51 N. 12TH ST., PHILADELPHIA

1. **PEARL'S OYSTER BAR**, **(215) 964-9792**

2. **DINIC'S ROAST PORK**, **(215) 923-6175**, tommydinics.com

3. **FLYING MONKEY BAKERY**, **(215) 928-0340**, flyingmonkeyphilly.com

4. **THE FAMOUS 4TH STREET COOKIE COMPANY**, **(215) 629-5990**,
   famouscookies.com

5. **BEILER'S DOUGHNUTS**, **(267) 318-7480**, beilersdoughnuts.com

Bonus Crawl!
Reading Terminal Market

Perhaps the most iconic food hall on the East Coast (at least if you ask anyone from the tri-state area), Reading Terminal Market is a true Philly institution. The market is the nation's oldest continuously operating farmer's market, dating all the way back to 1893. Nestled in the city's center, locals and tourists alike flock to Reading Terminal Market for everything from seafood to dessert to their weekly groceries.

1

PEARL'S OYSTER BAR

Start your feast at PEARL'S OYSTER BAR, which boasts some of the freshest seafood and has an excellent variety of oysters. Grab a sampler platter to start things off light. They source oysters from all over and have a wide variety for both the novice and expert consumer. They also do house-made soups, salads, and entrees featuring their fresh seafood.

2

DINIC'S ROAST PORK

Next, for a hearty bite, head to the center of the market to get a roast pork sandwich from **DINIC'S ROAST PORK**—heralded as one of the best sandwiches in Philadelphia. From the perfect Philly-style roll to the wonderfully salty, moist pork and creamy provolone, it's a sandwich that truly rivals the cheesesteak for Philly favorite. After your sandwich wander around the market while you digest, taking in the sights and checking out all of the local ven-

dors, selling everything from gourmet butter to local honey to produce to booze. Once your main course has settled, get ready for a seriously sweet stride through the market's dessert offerings.

3 FLYING MONKEY BAKERY

Start things off by heading over to FLY-ING MONKEY BAKERY for a slice of one of their rotating cakes (Sundae cake, anyone?!). You also must try the Pumpple Cake, which is as wild as it sounds. It starts with a layer of chocolate cake with an entire pumpkin pie baked inside. Then, that's topped with a vanilla cake layer with an entire apple pie baked inside, and then the entire cake is slathered in buttercream icing. It tastes like your holiday favorites combined with birthday cake, and is a decadent must-try at Reading Terminal Market.

4 THE FAMOUS 4TH STREET COOKIE COMPANY

Now onto THE FAMOUS 4TH STREET COOKIE COMPANY, where you can grab a cookie for later (trust me, they're perfectly soft and delicious, you'll want it as a midnight snack). Try a signature cookie—this sweet tooth recommends a classic chocolate chip (but they also have fun rotating flavors, like lemon coconut in the summer!).

5 BEILER'S DOUGHNUTS

Lastly, if you can stomach one more sweet bite (I promise, you can), then you must grab a donut from BEILER'S DOUGHNUTS on your way out. Beiler's is run by the Pennsylvania Dutch, owned and operated by the same family since 1984. Recipes have been passed down for generations, and thank goodness for that, because their donuts are some of the best in the city. They have around fifty varieties, so try whatever catches your eye, but this blogger highly recommends anything involving their peanut butter creme, which is light, fluffy, and full of nutty flavor.

THE WASHINGTON SQUARE WEST CRAWL

1. GREEN EGGS CAFÉ, 212 S. 13th St., Philadelphia, (267) 861-0314, greeneggscafe.com

2. MIDDLE CHILD, 248 S. 11th St., Philadelphia, (267) 930-8344, middlechildphilly.com

3. CRAFTSMAN ROW SALOON, 112 S. 8th St., Philadelphia, (215) 923-0123, craftsmanrowsaloon.com

4. SAMPAN, 124 S. 13th St., Philadelphia, (215) 732-3501, sampanphilly.com

5. INSOMNIA COOKIES, 135 S. 13th St., Philadelphia, (215) 544-2295, insomniacookies.com

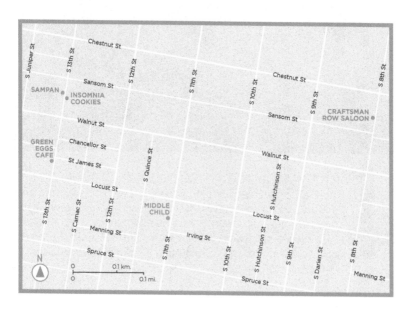

Washington Square West

Where Midtown meets the Gayborhood and we all win

Washington Square West is essentially the blending of Midtown Village and the Gayborhood, with Washington Square itself, one of Philly's original public squares, acting as a major landmark of the area. Midtown Village has tons of adorable local shops and restaurants, with 13th Street serving as the bustling epicenter and a favorite hangout for foodies. Gayborhood, clearly distinguished by the rainbow-painted sidewalks, boasts restaurants and bars just as fabulous as its residents. In Washington Square West you can catch couples strolling hand in hand as they peruse the local shops as well as groups of friends enjoying a decadent brunch outside at one of the many fantastic restaurants in the area. You may also see an occasional stressed-out doctor making their way over from Jefferson Hospital, jonesing for another cup of coffee to top off their shift. What's especially great about this neighborhood is that it caters to all of these people—those who want to shop, eat, or just want a quick stop to power through their day.

1 GREEN EGGS CAFÉ

GREEN EGGS CAFE is pretty much a Philadelphia institution, serving up crazy brunch dishes every day of the week. People flock here for their famous stuffed French toasts, crazy Benedicts, and cozy, laid-back atmosphere, and it's the perfect place to start your day of eating through Washington Square West.

TIP

They don't take reservations, so if you're coming on a weekend, prepare for a bit of a wait depending on group size.

Let's start this brunch savory by getting two of the most popular menu items—two totally different takes on a classic brunch dish—eggs Benedict. First off, the short rib Benedict. This Benny is anything but classic, as it has a base of two cheddar hash browns instead of a traditional English muffin, and is then topped with melt-in-your-mouth short rib, perfectly poached eggs, and a horseradish hollandaise. Let's follow this up with what may quickly become your favorite version of eggs Benny—the Chicken & Waffles Benedict. That's right, this dish features warm, sweet Belgian waffles, perfectly crispy fried chicken, and poached eggs on top, with maple syrup and hot sauce hollandaise.

Now, wipe that egg yolk off your face, because we've got one more dish here before we head out, and it happens to be the most popular dish for ten years running (and for good reason). I'm talking about crème brûlée French toast. This dish takes sliced challah bread, dips it in vanilla bean custard, fries it up so the edges are crispy but the center is soft, and tops it all with Chantilly cream and berries. Who says you can't have dessert for breakfast? Green Eggs Cafe is cash only.

2 MIDDLE CHILD

What if I told you that one of the best sandwiches you'll ever eat happens to be in Philly? Well, you're in luck, because in 2017 MIDDLE CHILD opened up and quickly took the breakfast and lunch scene by storm. The aesthetic is luncheonette meets Jewish deli meets hipster hangout—but don't let the simple facade fool you. At Middle Child they're making their own bread, their own sauce, their own meats (word on the street is that making their corned beef is a nine-day process).

TIP

Middle Child tends to sell out relatively early (by 2 p.m. or so), so the earlier you can get here, the better!

While they have salads and soups and other nice things (which are likely delicious), we didn't come to play—it's sandwich time. First off, it's important to note that they're often running specials, which you should probably get. These tend to be reflective of the season (turkey meatball cranberry gravy sub around Thanksgiving, etc.). However, for the purpose of this eating adventure, let's go with three menu items that are fan favorites and should (hopefully) still be there whenever you get your hands on this book. First, the Surfer.

This sandwich is piled high with turkey, Swiss arugula, mayo, and a healthy smattering of blueberry-masala jam on ciabatta for a fruity, delicate bite. Next, the Shopsin Club, which will make every other turkey club you've ever had pale in comparison. This sandwich has a mound of sliced turkey, Swiss, avocado, bacon, sweet pickles, lettuce, and cranberry miso mayo on a beautifully crispy ciabatta. Lastly, you must try a Reuben (Remember that corned beef that takes over a week to make? This is where it goes). The Reuben comes in corned beef or turkey varieties, both of which have Swiss, kraut, and a delicious secret sauce that takes it over the top (in the best way).

3 CRAFTSMAN ROW SALOON

You know when you see a food on Instagram that looks so crazy, so outrageous, that you can't help but say "wow"? That's basically the entire menu at **CRAFTSMAN ROW SALOON**. Put on your fat pants and get ready for some seriously sinful eats. From Mozzarella Stick Grilled Cheese to milkshakes with an entire slice of cake on them, Craftsman is not for the faint of heart. This laid-back bar on Jeweler's Row boasts an ever-changing menu catering to tourists and locals alike.

While you can definitely get decent standard bar fare here, take a walk on the wild side and get one of their riffs on a classic. Ditch the regular mozzarella sticks for their Doritos-crusted

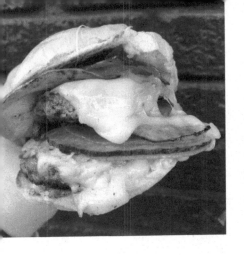

mozzarella sticks that are a pile of melty, double-cheesy goodness. Skip the regular burger and indulge in a double-patty mac-and-cheese burger (affectionately dubbed the Mac Daddy) and send a picture to all of your dieting friends. This burger features not one but two smashed house-made patties, topped with ooey-gooey homemade mac and cheese that takes it over the top (in the best way). Make sure you save room for some sweets here—their milkshakes are legendary in Philly. Whether you get them spiked or not, these shakes are perfect for sharing (since, you know, they're the size of your head). Even if it's not anywhere near your birthday, the Birthday Cake Shake is a slam dunk—piled high with candy, frosting, and sprinkles and topped with an entire slice of Funfetti Cake, this shake is a perfect sweet treat to end a decadent meal.

TIP

Ask them about their Instagram menu for some crazy concoctions that were basically created for the 'Gram.

4

SAMPAN

SAMPAN is a Pan-Asian restaurant with a menu composed of small and large plates, which makes it the perfect spot for a group outing. The menu is playful and inventive, and there's something for everyone, not to mention the space is super-cool. If you're coming here, the tasting menu is the way to go. You pick items from every section of the menu (small plates, satay, large plates, etc.) and everything will be portioned out according to the size of your group, so you don't have to worry about that awkward "four dumplings, five people" moment.

As far as specific dishes go, they're pretty much all delicious. The bao buns (which often change to keep things interesting) are

TIP

Sampan has one of the best happy hours in Philly, but get here super-early, as it always fills up!

always a hit. Imagine a tiny sandwich between pillowy soft, lightly sweet steamed buns for the perfect vehicle for whatever filling is inside. The Korean BBQ Beef Satay is exquisite—beef is sliced razor thin and rolled up on skewers in a pungent, flavorful sauce. The crispy rock shrimp is creamy, sweet, spicy, crunchy, and tangy (from the pickled radish) all in one—talk about umami. As a side, definitely get the pad Thai, which has shrimp, chopped-up egg, tofu, and peanut (and is more of a main dish than a side). For your meat, the duck bao buns are a super-fun DIY entree. Take the piece of perfectly cooked duck, put it in the tiny scallion-steamed bun, and top with your desired sauces and veggies. Lastly, for dessert the tasting menu comes with mini cones of Sampan's house-made ice cream, which changes flavor often (but is always delicious!).

5 INSOMNIA COOKIES

In 2003 Seth Berkowitz, a college student at the University of Pennsylvania, started INSOMNIA COOKIES as a way to feed the insatiable sweet tooth of the greater college student population, and the brand has since exploded, growing to more than one hundred locations. Given that Insomnia was born in Philadelphia, it's only right that you try one of their delicious cookies before wrapping up this food crawl, and lucky for you, there's a location right on 13th Street.

Insomnia offers more than just cookies—brownies, ice cream, etc.—but the cookies are really the star here. There are two cookie categories: traditional and deluxe. Traditional are your more standard-sized, standard-flavor treats, whereas deluxe are big, over-the top cookies. You can probably guess which ones I'm going to recommend. . . .

When it comes to deluxe cookies, there is no wrong choice. The Reese's Peanut Butter Cup one has an entire Reese's baked into a peanut butter cookie and literally melts in your mouth with heavenly notes of chocolate and peanut butter. The S'mores cookie is a chocolate-based cookie with chocolate, marshmallow, and graham crackers in it, and it tastes like sitting around a campfire with your friends on a summer night making s'mores. The Chocolate Chunk is a classic—ooey-gooey chocolate goodness. The best part of Insomnia (besides the fact that most locations are open super-late) is that cookies are served warm, so you can always have that fresh-from-the-oven satisfaction.

BONUS CRAWL! JUST DESSERTS

1. **CAKE LIFE BAKE SHOP**, 1306 Frankford Ave., Philadelphia, (215) 278-2580, cakelifebakeshop.com

2. **WECKERLY'S ICE CREAM**, 9 W. Girard Ave., Philadelphia, (215) 423-2000, weckerlys.com

3. **FEDERAL DONUTS**, 701 N. 7th St., Philadelphia, (267) 928-3893, federaldonuts.com

4. **THE BAKESHOP ON TWENTIETH**, 269 S. 20th St., Philadelphia, (215) 644-9714, bakeshopon20th.com

5. **SWEET BOX**, 339 S. 13th St., Philadelphia, (215) 237-4647, shopsweetbox.com

6. **ISGRO PASTRIES**, 1009 Christian St., Philadelphia, (215) 923-3092, isgropastries.com

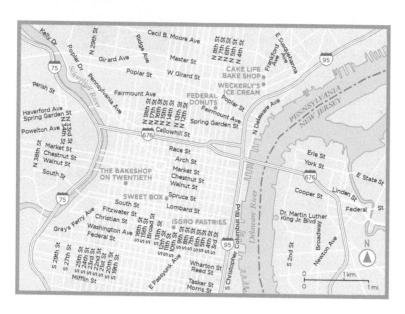

Bonus Crawl! Just Desserts

If you have a sweet tooth and a hankering to see Philadelphia's various neighborhoods from top to bottom, then this is a crawl for you. Philadelphia is known for its bustling food and drink scene, but did you know that Philly also cranks out world-class baked goods? From cakes to cannolis, donuts to the infamous "Jawn" cookie dough/cake/frosting bar, the desserts coming out of the City of Brotherly Love will have you abandoning your diet real quick. You can't eat dessert all day if you don't start in the morning. Start this crawl early, as many bakeries tend to close by midday.

1 CAKE LIFE BAKE SHOP

If you look up "girl power" in the dictionary, you'll probably find a picture of CAKE LIFE BAKE SHOP. Run by a female-led management team, this bakery is woman-owned and trans-owned, and they're damn proud of it. When owners Lily and Nima, best friends since they met in their freshman year of college, had quarter-life crises, they decided to quit their careers and head to pastry school. After winning Food Network's *Cupcake Wars*, they decided to open a commercial bakery in the heart of Fishtown.

Cake Life Bake Shop has made Beyoncé's birthday cake—twice! Queen Bee herself loves their gorgeous cake creations so much that when she's in town for her birthday, she gets a crazy custom cake made.

Since this is your first stop of the day, it's essentially breakfast (the best part of adulthood is that cake for breakfast is completely acceptable). Start with one of their homemade Pop-Tarts, which have a crispy sugar outside, flaky puff pastry, and delicious fruity filling. Next, the Honey Sea Salt Tart is the perfect mix of sweet and a hint of salty, and the honey flavor truly shines. And finally—cake.

They serve all of their cakes by the slice, so you can grab a few to try. The Red Velvet is perfectly executed—moist, dense cake layers with a tangy cream-cheese frosting, laid on thick. The Funfetti Cake will have you feeling like a kid again, with fluffy vanilla cake, light buttercream frosting, and confetti sprinkles. Lastly, Cake Life Bake Shop has rotating Cakes of the Month, which you should absolutely try. They're typically a unique combination of flavors that are reflective of the season (like the pictured Pistachio Rose cake). As you lick the frosting off the plate (no judgment), get ready for the next stop in this sweet crawl.

2 WECKERLY'S ICE CREAM

WECKERLY'S is as hand-made as ice cream gets. Everything is sourced from local farms, no mixes are used, and flavors are ever-changing to reflect what's seasonal. This micro-creamery specializes in small-batch, unique ice cream flavors that are inspired by Philadelphia and rooted in classic French technique. Driven by a love of pastry and deep respect for local farmers, Jen Satinsky, a trained pastry chef, and her husband, Andy, opened Weckerly's in 2012.

The first thing you should try here is a scoop of ice cream on a cone—pretty simple, but you really need to have the ice cream on its own to appreciate the complexity of flavors and the smooth silky texture. Next, you must try one of their ice cream sandwiches, which are iconically square. Pictured are lemon ice cream sandwiches, with a strip of blackberry jam in the center, on sugar cookies. The ice cream sandwiches are constantly changing, from the ice cream flavor to the filling to the cookie, so grab whatever sounds good to you. Lastly, you can have the best of both worlds by getting a scoop of ice cream *and* a mini ice cream sandwich. Not only does it make for an adorable, Instagrammable treat, but it lets you try two completely different things in one tasty package.

3

FEDERAL DONUTS

FEDERAL DONUTS just proves that there's nothing Mike Solomonov can't do. From Zahav (one of the nation's best restaurants; find it in the Old City Crawl) to Abe Fisher (an amazing dinner; in the Rittenhouse Crawl) to Dizengoff (the best hummus ever; in the Vegan Crawl), Solomonov has helped to transform the Philly dining scene. Federal Donuts is one of the sweeter notches on his belt, as he is also the mastermind behind some of Philly's favorite donuts.

The menu at Federal Donuts is straightforward, yet unexpected—mostly because they also sling some seriously delicious fried chicken, but that's a treat for another day—we're here for donuts. There are three donuts that are available year-round—Cookies and Cream, Cinnamon Brown Sugar, and Strawberry

Lavender sugar donuts are prepared hot and fresh every day. They're dense, unfilled, and full of flavor. There are also Fancy Donuts, which rotate regularly to reflect what's in season. Think Pumpkin Spice Latte donut in the fall, Snow Cap donut in the winter, Lemon Meringue donut in the summer, etc. These are the real stars of the show—the fancy donuts do not skimp on flavor or toppings, and you can try something new every time you go back (because, trust me, you're going to want to go back).

4 THE BAKESHOP ON TWENTIETH

Your next stop is a quaint little storefront on 20th Street that's creating scratch-made goodness every day. Owned by Lisa and Mark Cosgrove, this bakery specializes in small-batch, inventive versions of classic baked goods, with a heavy focus on what's in season. In addition to baked goods, they offer made-to-order sandwiches, in case you have a hankering for something salty amid all this sweet.

BAKESHOP is definitely the place to get a cookie—they have some of the city's best. The Chocolate Chip Tahini cookie is reminiscent of a childhood favorite but elevated by the nutty flavor of sesame from the tahini. The Iced Oatmeal Raisin cookie is a perfect rendition of a classic, with ribbons of sweet icing draped over a chewy, soft oatmeal base, dotted with sweet, tart raisins. If you're feeling adventurous, try whatever the special cookie is—like the pictured Double Dark Chocolate Mint, which is reminiscent of a mint brownie, in cookie form. Lastly, if cookies aren't your thing, they have an array of other delicious treats, such as their babka or their scones. Scone flavors tend to rotate as well, and if you happen to land here in the fall, the Pumpkin Scone is excellent.

Hope your sweet tooth isn't hurting yet, because there are even more treats on the horizon!

5

SWEET BOX

Is SWEET BOX one of Philly's favorite bakeries? You *batter* believe it. If there's one thing they know here—it's dough (cookie dough, that is!). This charming little shop on 13th Street makes outrageously delicious edible cookie dough, fifteen-plus cupcake flavors, and a cookie dough–cake frosting hybrid called the Jawn.

When you visit Sweet Box, you must try their edible cookie dough in one of its many forms. The simplest is by the scoop, but what's the fun in simple? Get a cookie dough pop, which looks like a Popsicle but spares you the brain freeze,

since it's sweet, chewy edible cookie dough covered in a thick chocolate shell. Next, try it sandwiched between two soft sugar cookies. How about cookie dough on a decadent chocolate brownie, with a thick layer of chocolate on top? Yeah, they have that too. Lastly, you cannot leave without trying the outrageous, infamous Jawn. The OG Jawn has a Funfetti Cake base, topped with cookie dough and buttercream icing. It was such a viral hit that Sweet Box has since created Cookies and Cream and Chocolate Peanut Butter versions (and honestly, you should try them all).

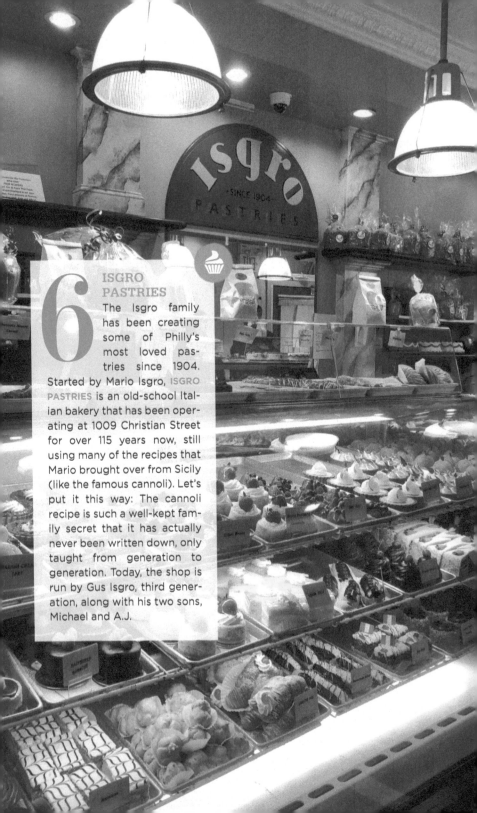

6 ISGRO PASTRIES

The Isgro family has been creating some of Philly's most loved pastries since 1904. Started by Mario Isgro, ISGRO PASTRIES is an old-school Italian bakery that has been operating at 1009 Christian Street for over 115 years now, still using many of the recipes that Mario brought over from Sicily (like the famous cannoli). Let's put it this way: The cannoli recipe is such a well-kept family secret that it has actually never been written down, only taught from generation to generation. Today, the shop is run by Gus Isgro, third generation, along with his two sons, Michael and A.J.

While you may not be able to re-create the Isgro cannoli, you can definitely eat it, and that should be your first order of business here. The shell is perfectly crispy and lightly sweet, and the filling is a rich, smooth ricotta, dotted with chocolate chips for that little something extra (you can get other cannoli flavors as well). Next, try their famous cheesecake, which you

can get as an entire cake (they run a serious cake business) or as an individual mini cake. The cheesecake is dense, thick, tangy, and sweet—as a perfect cheesecake should be, sitting on a moist graham base, topped with a dollop of whipped cream and a fresh strawberry. Lastly, Isgro's is famous for their Italian rum cake, which is made with a generous amount of real rum. This cake is filled with creamy ricotta and topped with sliced almonds, for a true taste of Italy in every bite.

TIP

Isgro made pastries for Pope Francis during his visit to Philadelphia for the World Meeting of the Families in 2016. They provided him with cake and pastries during his stay in Philadelphia as well as to take back to Rome.

Index

About the Author

Jacklin Altman is the mind behind Philly-based blog and Instagram foodbythe gram.com/@foodbythegram. She can usually be found in the kitchen baking or hovering over her brunch to get the best possible picture of it. Raised just outside of Philadelphia, she moved into the city in 2011, and it can't seem to get rid of her since. She's watched food trends from far and wide make their way to Philly and has seen the food scene explode as more and more talented chefs, restau-rateurs, and bakers alike have decided to call Philly home. Jacklin is passion-ate about new and unique cuisines and will proudly eat anything that doesn't eat her first. She's always trying out the city's newest, craziest, and most Insta-grammable eats and treats and sharing them with her Instagram followers.